THE NAKED EDGE

THE NAKED EDGE

The Complete Guide to Edged Weapons Defense

STEVE TARANI

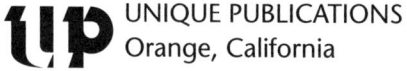
UNIQUE PUBLICATIONS
Orange, California

Disclaimer

Please note that the author and publisher of this book are NOT RESPONSIBLE in any manner whatsoever for any injury that may result from practicing the techniques and/or following the instructions given within. Since the physical activities described herein may be too strenuous in nature for some readers to engage in safely, it is essential that a physician be consulted prior to training.

Warning

Always train with training weapons only! Under no circumstances should training with real edged weapons be attempted.

First published in 2002 by Unique Publications.

Copyright © 2002 by CFW Enterprises, Inc.

All rights reserved. No part of this publication may be reproduced or utilized in any form or by any means, electronic or mechanical, including photocopying, recording, or by any information storage and retrieval system, without prior written permission from Unique Publications.

Library of Congress Catalog Number: 2002012710
ISBN: 0-86568-207-0

Unique Publications
265 S. Anita Dr. Ste. 120
Orange, CA 92868
(800) 332–3330
Second edition
05 04 03 02 01 00 99 98 97 1 3 5 7 9 10 8 6 4 2

Printed in the United States of America

Editor: John S. Soet
Design: Patrick Gross
Cover Design: George Chen

Dedication

*This book is dedicated with honor and loving respect
to the memory of my Filipino Eskrima Masters
Grandmaster Leovigildo Miguel Giron
and Punong Guro Edgar G. Sulite
Da'ghan Ka'yong Salamat sa Duha Na'ko ka Maestros*

Foreword

Welcome to *The Naked Edge: The Complete Guide to Edged Weapons Defense*. This book is intended to introduce the fundamentals of Edged Weapons Defensive Technology including the demonstration and instruction of the gross motor skills necessary to handling an edged weapon attack at contact range.

When under stress an individual will fall back upon those fundamentals that they are conditioned to execute. Conditioning comes from many repetitions and many repetitions is just another term for conditioning training. Thus, the secret to proficiency in defensive tactics against edged weapon attacks is simply repetitions.

> *"Repetition is the mother of all skills."*
> —Punong Guro Edgar G. Sulite

Although the majority of this text is geared toward empty-hand defense against a knife attack, there are certain situations where a student is presented with various aspects of operating a knife. With this type of training comes a moral and ethical responsibility. Those of us who choose to carry a knife must also carry the responsibility to train with it. The material in this manuscript is compiled for that purpose and with the intention of self-defense application only.

Acknowledgements

Humbly, I would like to extend my most sincere gratitude to Grandmaster Leo M. Giron, Punong Guro Edgar G. Sulite, the entire Sulite family, Guro Dan Inosanto, Master Rey Galang, Master Christopher Ricketts, Master Antonio Diego, Master Tony Somera, Guro Dexter Labanog, Guro Glenn Abrescy, and all of the Bahala Na Stockton group and Bakbakan International.

Additionally, I would like to personally thank the entire core group of the original SCEA: David Hines, Barry Shreiar, Paul "Bubba" "Ted" Grybow, Tim Egberts, Mike Doctulero, Tim Lau, Romi Archer, Jim Johnson and Jerry McGinnis for their unconditional support throughout the years as well as Ben Salas and Brian Everett for their contributions to this project.

Contents

Part One—The fundamentals of Edged Weapons Defense Technology

History of the Knife—Prehistoric and Ancient 2
    High Middle Ages through the Elizabethan Age 5
    The Rest of the World 9
    In America 10
The Importance of Edged Weapon Training 14
Choosing the Best 17
    Training Knives 21
Basic Training Terminology 27
Anatomy of Attack and Defense 31
    Control of Body Position 32
    Distance, Timing, and Reaction 34
    Mobility 38
Carry and Deployment 42
Closing Your Folding Knife 47
Grips 48
Edged Weapon Attacks 52
Defensive Hand Postures 53
Gross Motor Skills 55
    Turn One Way 56
    QuickShield™ 56
    Body Pivots 58

Part Two—Defending Against Non-Contact and Contact Range Attacks

Break and Clear (Non-Contact Range) 66
Move to the Outside 70
Defending Against Contact Range Attacks 72
    Down and Away Drills 73
    High Line Attacks 77

Elbow Control 80
    Pain Compliance versus Mechanical Compliance 82
    Opposing Strengths 84
    Elbow Control Problem Solving 91
    The Next Step 100
Elbow Control (High Line Attacks) 101

PART THREE—DEFENSE AND DISARMING AT EXTREME CLOSE QUARTERS (ECQ)

Rear Obstructions 112
ECQ Footwork 113
    Elements of ECQ Footwork 113
ECQ Handwork 118
Safety Hand 122
    The "C"-Clamp 122
Cross-Body 131
Disarms—No Remaining Options 139
Father of the Four Fingers 139
Meeting and Following 141
Classical Disarming of an Edged Weapon 141
Reverse Grip Inside Disarm 141
    Reverse Grip Inside Disarm Option 144
Closing the Car Door Disarm (Forearm Strip) 147
C-Clamp Leg Strip 150
Cross Body Feed Ramp Strip 152

Bibliography 155
Contact Weapons Street Survival Formula 157
    Street Survival Table 158
About the Author 163

PART ONE

THE FUNDAMENTALS OF EDGED WEAPONS DEFENSE TECHNOLOGY

History of the Knife—Prehistoric and Ancient

Researchers, relying upon archeological evidence, have isolated the birthplace of the knife and dagger somewhere in the northeast corner of the ancient African continent. The evolution of these weapons can be traced from the European Stone Age, with significant modification in design, material and functionality, throughout the ancient Middle East, ancient Greece, ancient Rome, Medieval Europe, 16th century Europe, the Pacific Island peoples, 17th Century Europe, 18th Century America, the French Revolution Wars, the American Civil War, both World Wars and all the way up to and including our modern nuclear age.

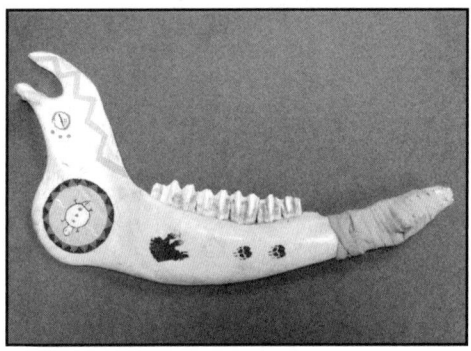

Replica of very early Native American jawbone axe-knife.

The earliest recorded archeological evidence for prehistoric edged weapon combat was discovered during the early 1960's at a burial site along the Nile River in ancient Nubia, located between Egypt and Ethiopia. The site contains remnants of several dozen human bodies dating from approximately between 12,000 and 8,000 BC. The archeological record indicates that between these same dates there was a revolution in weapons technology. During this period four new weapons made their first appearance: the bow, the sling, the mace and last, but certainly not least, the knife and dagger.

About forty percent of these remains were found buried along side small bone flake points and a number of points found still embedded in some of the bones. Although no cogent evidence was uncovered via written record, researchers have observed that several individuals appeared to have been executed. Additionally several of the skeletons had fractured arms in such a manner as consistent with warding off heavy impact strikes at close quarter range thus indicating struggle.

Part One—The Fundamentals of Edged Weapons Defense Technology

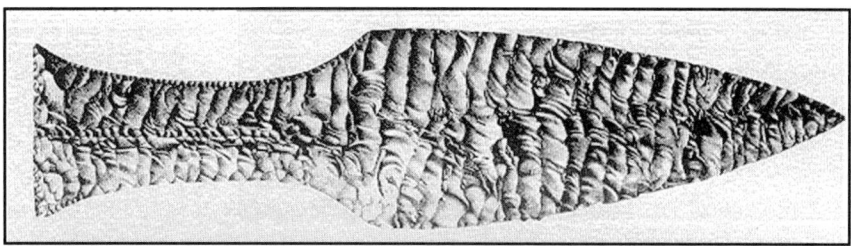

Stone Age Flint Knife

Cave paintings such as the ones of Lascaux, France and Teruel, Spain, which date as far back as 25,000 to 15,000 BC, illustrate possible evidence of man's earliest weapons. Prehistoric hunters equipped themselves with such weapons to ensure basic survival. To convert those same weapons on their own kind was a simple step if, much like modern politics, the ends justified the means. Small hunting and gathering groups that weathered the last ice age had cause on occasion to attack each other for dominion over valuable resources like food, water and important raw materials. This is from where the old saying comes "he who has the weapons makes the rules."

Although modern synthetic materials and stainless steel may have replaced the stone and bone blades of old, a knife and dagger of today's modern mechanized society is just as deadly as the knife and dagger of the ancient stone-age village.

Obsidian Antler Daggers

There are basically two types of knives and daggers. They are fixed (that knife or dagger which has no moving parts), and folding which can have as many as five or more moving parts.

The first folding knives date from as far back as the late part of the Roman Empire (circa 2nd-4th century AD). Today we often refer to them as "pocket knives", but their invention and use actually predates that of the sewn on pocket.

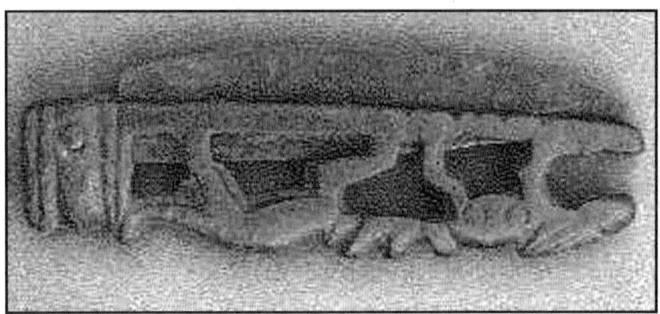

Ancient Roman Folding Knife

The earliest known folding knives had no back springs in their handles. Reliable, crucible cast spring steel wouldn't be produced until 1742 as the invention of a clock maker in Sheffield, England named B.A. Huntsman. Interestingly enough, inexpensive folding knives to this very day are made in the ancient Roman style without back springs!

Inclusion of the dagger as part and parcel of military accoutrements, continued from the late Roman Empire (c. 540 AD) on through the Middle Ages.

Part One—The Fundamentals of Edged Weapons Defense Technology

High Middle Ages through the Elizabethan Age

Although the knife and dagger were considered secondary weapons (as the sword dominated the battlefield as a primary weapon throughout the ancient world), they were essential to the armory of some of the most powerful armies of antiquity. In fact, from the earliest times of issued body armor in the 3rd quarter of the 14th century, the dagger became an indispensable and visible part of a warrior's equipment.

Le Moyne's Sketches

Famous tapestries of old such as the Bayeux tapestry, details from Le Moyne's sketches of the French in Florida in 1564 and just about every military monument from that era displays a dagger of one type or another. Many civilian figures are also depicted wearing knives and daggers, which were as popular with citizens then, as our high-tech combat folding knives are to us now.

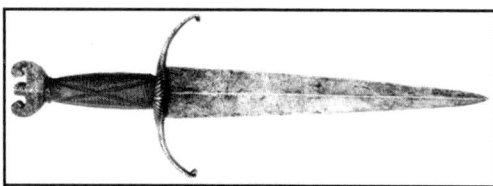

Early Quillon Style Dagger c.15th Century

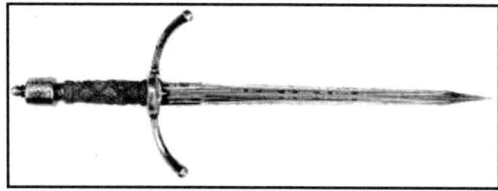

Quillon c.1560

The 15th century saw the development of knife fighting elevated to that of an art form. Man had evolved and so too had his skills. What had begun as a tool had become a weapon. What was merely a weapon had become an art. European techniques and tactics rivaled those of their Asian brethren.

16th Century German Manuscript

In ancient Europe, during the Elizabethan era, dueling was at the height of its popularity among the gentry' class. The rapier (long, thin sword predominantly used for thrusting) and dagger (sometimes referred to as *main gauche*) was the most popular weapon system of the day. Certain scholars claim that the number of civilians dueling with the rapier and dagger reached epidemic proportions by the end of the 16th century. In those days, professional schools of fencing could be readily found in any metropolitan area. Thus, in order to employ the deadly "tools of the duel" with any efficiency, a potential duelist needed a minimum number of hours of hard training each day for the simple preservation of his life, and his honor.

The primary elements of this sophisticated swordsmanship, as indicated by the ancient masters of fence in that era, were balance and timing. Balance, according to the masters, was defined as "stability produced by even distribution of weight on either side of center bodily mass." Timing, however, was simply defined as being in the right place at the right time.

Part One—The Fundamentals of Edged Weapons Defense Technology

These same masters of fence emphasized the ever-important essentials of balance and timing when handling both the rapier and the dagger.

According to European fencing manuscripts, dating as far back as the mid-1400's, certain techniques were developed to take advantage of your opponent should he be found off balance and/ or out of position (i.e. in the wrong place at the wrong time). Even today, the masters of modern edged-weapon training emphasize the repetition of training drills that engage and develop timing and balance.

Elizabethan era example of Rapier and Dagger fighting posture.

Technological advances in metallurgy and combative tactics had changed drastically during the Elizabethan era. Influential European fencing masters such as Giacomo DiGrassi and Vincentio Saviolo published their discoveries that the thrust was found to be superior to the slash. These discoveries validated the ancient Roman writings of Flavius Vegetus Renetus who noted that the Roman generals found that the thrust was superior to the slash and thus was the basis for adaptation of the Roman *Gladius* (thrusting sword). Thus, swords and sword fighting techniques changed from double-handed slashers to single handed thrusters and almost always accompanied by the *main gauche*—(literal translation of the old French meaning "left hand") the predecessor to the modern carry combat folder.

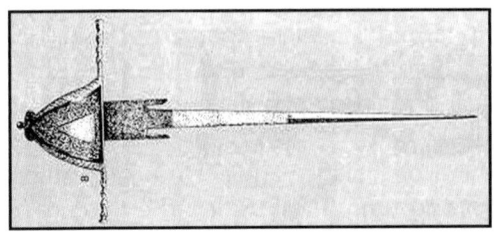 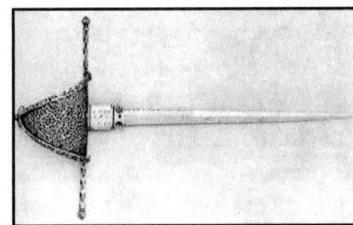

Main Gauche

Fighting systems developed employing the use of both the sword and dagger, such as the well-known Spanish *Espada Y Daga* system. Such fighting systems were made popular during the Spanish conquests of the Philippine Islands during the early 16th century although evidence points to such systems in existence around the time of the battle of Hastings in 1066 AD. In addition, the newly developed thrusting implements (rapiers and main gauche) were employed for dueling up to and throughout the late 19th century even in America.

As necessity is the mother of invention, the dagger developed over the years and assumed different shapes and styles such as the Basilard dagger and the Rondel Dagger.

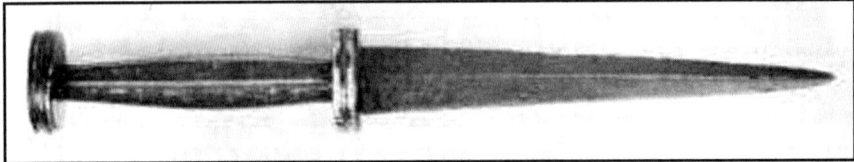

Rondel Type Dagger

These types were the basic types of dagger used in Europe during the period 1350-1500, but we can't neglect mention of the famous Italian Stiletto; a purely stabbing weapon with absolutely no cutting edge. The Stiletto was commonplace, feared and respected in Italy and throughout Europe during the 17th and 18th centuries.

Part One—The Fundamentals of Edged Weapons Defense Technology

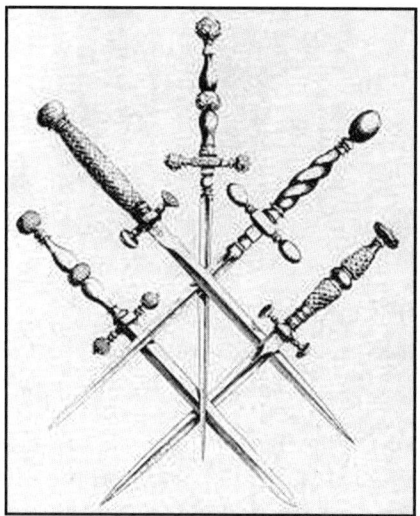

Italian Stiletto Types

The Rest of the World

Development of the knife and dagger and the fighting systems by which they were employed were being simultaneously developed in such locations as Australia, New Zealand, Polynesia, the Indonesian Archipelago, Southeast Asia, China, Burma, Assam, Thailand, Japan, India and Persia, Africa, and the Americas.

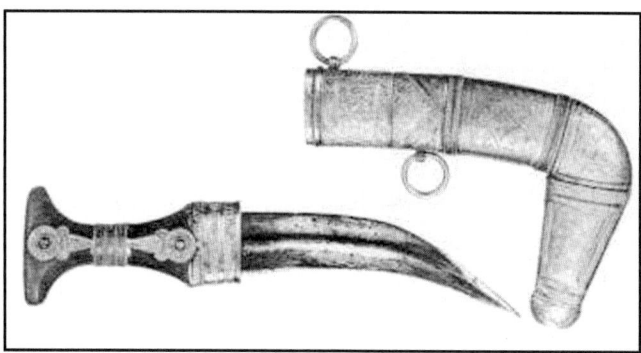

Jambiya Style Blade

Jambiya from North Africa, an Arab dagger found in many variations by the mid-19th century. All have a curved double-edged blade.

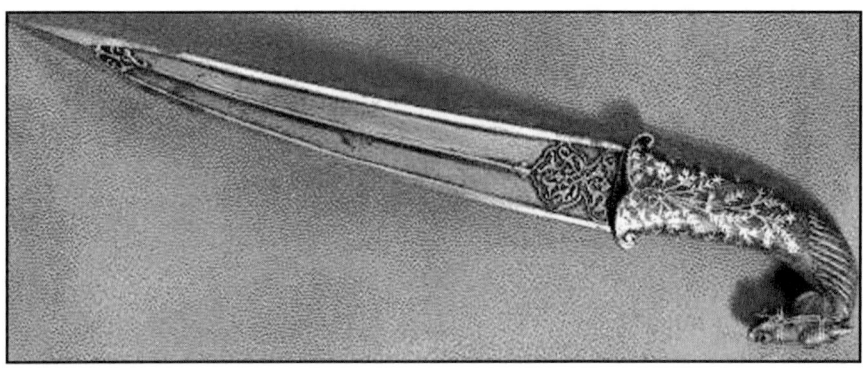

Indian Khanjar

Descendants of the ancient Indus Valley (modern day India) witnessed the development of a dagger known as the Khanjar. India, with its rich and diverse history of armed combat and weapon development, greatly influenced the design and functionality of the weapons of Malaysia, Indonesia and even the Philippines as a result of migrations Eastward.

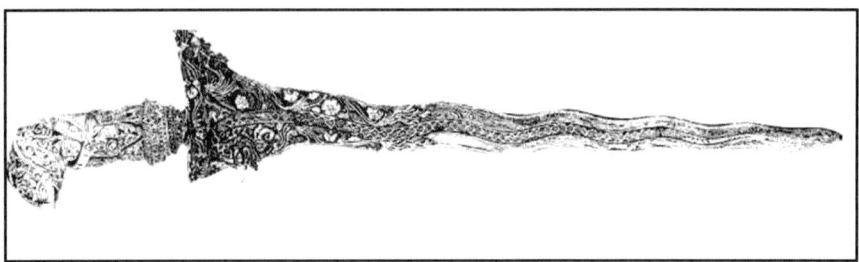

Malaysian Kris c. 1600

The "tongue of fire" blade shape characterizes The Kris from Malaysia and Indonesia. It is considered a very sacred blade sometimes believed to posses magical powers.

IN AMERICA
In the Americas, notwithstanding brief visits of the Vikings amidst the 9th century, there was a stretch of about 500 years when no European knives or daggers were carried to America. The development of Native

American blades was left to flourish pretty much untainted until the mid-16th century.

Somewhere around 1505, just after the turn of the century, Spanish influx began in the South and Southwest Americas. Records of these early Spanish expeditions take daggers for granted and fail to provide intimate detail of the exact types used. Several types of daggers were popular in Spain at the time and were thus standard issue to the likes of Conquistadors, explorers and their armories. These were the Eared Dagger, the Rondel Dagger and the Quillon Dagger to name a few.

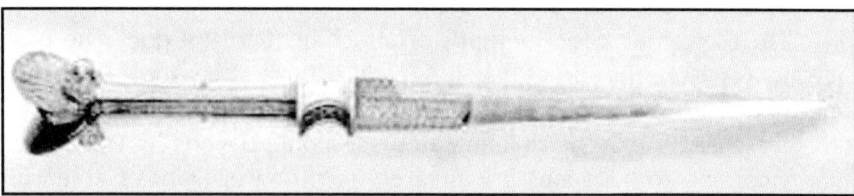

Eared Dagger

Certain exotic weapons were also produced such as push daggers. Nothing new in the world of edged weapons as the push dagger had been around in India for centuries, however, these had an American flair and became somewhat common during the American Civil War.

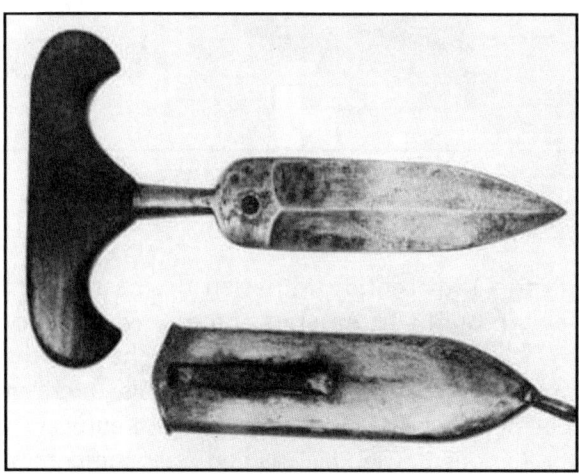

Civil War Push Dagger

After 1650 one type of dagger distinguishable in America was the plug bayonet. A bayonet is defined as any blade that can be affixed to the muzzle of a gun. In its original and primary role, it quickly converts an infantry musket into a pike or spear. During the mid to late 1600's, ranks of pike-men were employed to protect musketeers against cavalry while reloading. The bayonet allowed a musketeer to defend himself as he now had a pike in hand. The vast majority of 17th century infantry were trained in the use of long bayonets. Since World War I, however, there was a change in philosophy regarding use of the bayonet. By the end of war, most armies adopted short bayonets with the added useful secondary feature as a general-purpose knife.

There are four basic methods of attachment to the gun: The plug bayonet (1640's), the socket bayonet (early 1700's), the sword/ knife bayonet (late 18th century) and the Dahlgren bayonet (19th century). The first recognized use in the United States was a plug bayonet of French origin. According to historians it was taken from one of France's American Indian allies near Deerfield, Massachusetts in 1675. The plug bayonet remained popular until circa 1700 when it was then replaced by the socket bayonet.

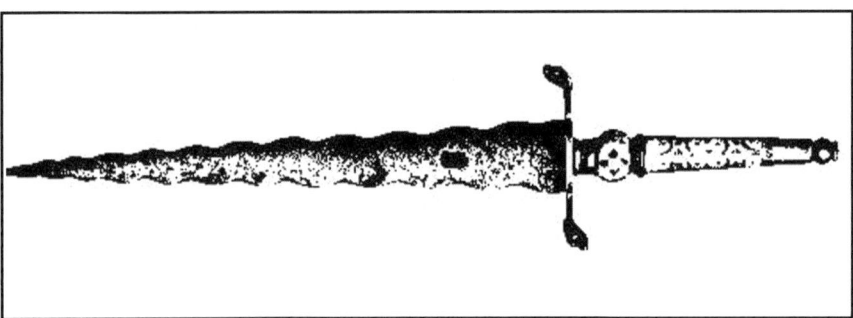

17 Century English plug bayonet

Although the 18th century witnessed the passing of the old plug bayonet, it also brought to America some new and very interesting knives. These included the Scottish Dirk—brought over the Atlantic by hordes of immigrating Scots in the 1730's and 40's, the rifleman's knife—used to cut patches of grease cloth to load the "Kentucky" rifle, and the creation of the famous Bowie knife named after the commander of the forces at the Alamo who died there in 1836 with the rest of the garrison.

PART ONE—THE FUNDAMENTALS OF EDGED WEAPONS DEFENSE TECHNOLOGY

Rumor has it that Bowie used to hang around with Filipino sailors who traveled to the Americas and that it was his penchant for Filipino cutlery that influenced the design of the knife which bears his namesake.

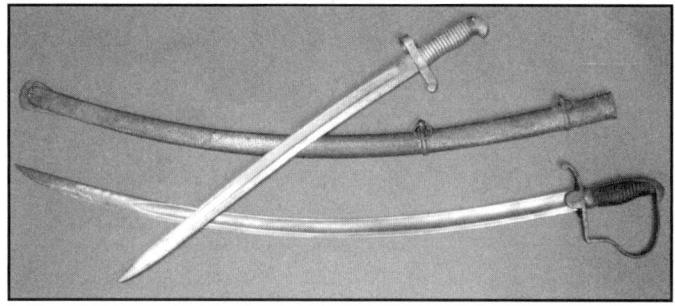

American Revolution Officer's Saber and Scabbard with Civil War era Bayonet.

Other popular knives like the Ames rifleman's knife of 1849, the US Army hunting knife of 1880 and the new Hospital Corps Knife of 1904, brought about the modern development of the knife and dagger that carries through to manufacture and designs of today.

During the Spanish-American war around 1898 and throughout the American occupation of the Philippine Islands, it became necessary for a heavy knife that could be used for both fighting and clearing a path through thick undergrowth. The U.S. Army, officially adapted this blade already invented and employed by the native Filipino's centuries earlier, in 1904.

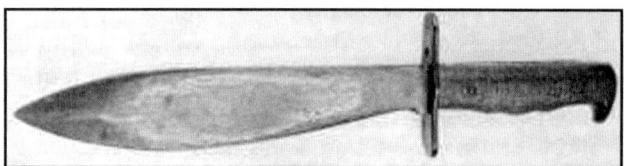

American Bolo c.1900

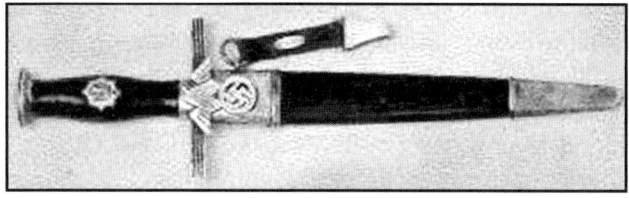

Nazi Ceremonial Dagger c.1939

The Importance of Edged Weapon Training

Circa 3rd century BC, the brutally effective battle phalanx of the Macedonian army was comprised of individual warriors armed with a sarissa (heavy spear). Varying in lengths from 9 to 21 feet the sarissa had a really long reach and could easily pierce the shields and breastplates of any enemy in its deadly path. Although devastating when used in mass warfare, the sarissa was heavy and unwieldy, thus unsuitable for fighting man to man. For this purpose each Macedonian warrior was armed with a small sword called a kopus, which was his primary backup, when it got up close and personal.

The ancient Roman Legions were armed with two pila (short spears) and a gladius (sword). Formidable as he was, these primary weapons systems were sometimes either lost or rendered disabled in the natural course of bloody combat. In such cases he had the security of knowing that he could rely upon his primary backup—the pugio (Roman dagger) and his superior training.

All throughout history warriors and civilians alike have depended upon both primary and secondary weapon systems as well as their training in each for both warring en masse and in personal defense.

What the kopus was to the sarissa (Greek), the pugio to the gladius (Roman), the main gauche to the sabre (French), the daga to the espada (Spanish), the dirk to the basket hilt (Scottish), the wakazashi to the katana (Japan), the dagger to the rapier (English), is what is akin to all weapon systems—primary backup.

All the way up to and including the Revolutionary and Civil Wars in America and the global conflict of both world wars, the fighting man had at his disposal both a primary and secondary weapon system. This can be observed in our own modern law enforcement and military units. Any special operations unit personnel are well-trained and armed with both a primary (i.e. carbine, rifle, shotgun or sub-gun) and secondary (small-bore semi-automatic pistol—.45, .40, 9mm, etc.,). You would also be hard pressed to find any special operations unit personnel without a knife clipped or strapped on to some part of his body armor.

Civilian fixed blades, folding knives, daggers, stilettos, push-daggers and neck-knives have existed for as long as personal combat has been around. During Elizabethan times, a properly trained English gentleman was armed with both his rapier and accompanying dagger even at the most formal of social affairs. During the same era a French magistrate

Part One—The Fundamentals of Edged Weapons Defense Technology

wouldn't be caught dead without his main gauche slung gracefully as an accoutrement to his fine wardrobe.

Today some of us are fortunate enough to live in a state of the union enabling its citizens personal defense via carry or ownership of a firearm. Some of us, however, are quite unfortunate in that certain state legislation, a county sheriff or local police chief would rather you sit at home defenseless while your family is violated by intruders, than legally enable you to stand strong against the criminal element in self-defense with a firearm or edged weapon.

Training in combative application with a firearm is hard enough to find, but how can we possibly expect knife-owners—who carry their blades as primary backup—to learn how to properly and safely, handle, operate and maintain their knives?

If you were elbow to elbow in one of the ancient Roman legions marching with your sword drawn and shield raised head on into the fray of battle, you would have nothing but your equipment and your training to depend upon for your survival. The same if you were part of an elite commando unit or a special operations team. It boils down to the two most important aspects of weapons systems—your hardware and your training.

What's the difference between yourself and an ancient Macedonian warrior when you find yourself in a life and death self-defense confrontation in the street? There you are standing face to face in harms way, your primary weapon system is unavailable. Armed with only your primary backup, would you truly feel confident and capable in your hardware and in your training?

Training in edged weapons defense has always been a primary consideration from the ancient Spartans all the way down through the annals of history to the present day.

Personal combat with edged weapons has been around as long as there has been a life and death struggle between two adversaries and is as old as the hills. As opposed to mass warfare, personal combat is generally close quarter, one-on-one, hand-to-hand, up close and personal.

Over the centuries, personal combat took on many different forms. During these early times, edged weapons were considered king of personal combat. By the 1500s personal armed conflicts were part of everyday life. According to contemporary British historians "Seldom shall you see one of my countrymen above eighteen years old go without a dagger at least at his back or side." As weapons became more streamlined, the styles for fighting on a personal level grew more refined and potentially deadlier. During the 18th century sword and dagger handling had reached unsurpassed efficiency. The introduction of repeating firearms virtually ended the value of hand-held blades as a military weapon and the primary choice for personal combat. The knife and dagger were then relegated only as a backup to the indiscriminate and impersonal firearm.

The grim reality of personal combat with an edged weapon is that you can get deeply cut by a razor's edged or skewered by a sharp point. The level of skill in proficiency required to be successful in an edged weapon encounter is far beyond that of a boxer, grappler or kickboxer. You may be able to survive a right cross to the jaw or a straight arm-bar, or possibly a round kick to the ribs, however, you may not make it through an ear-to-ear slash across your throat or a punctured spleen.

Personal combat with an edged weapon is truly nasty business. If someone pulls out a knife and attacks you with it, you're already behind the power curve. Reaction is always slower than action. You could never respond as fast as or faster than a first strike.

Do you really want to get into it with someone knife against knife? Have you ever "play sparred" with a training partner to see what it was like to go at it knife to knife? Or what about empty hand versus knife?

One of the best training drills designed to simulate an edged weapon personal combat experience, is to have both your partner and yourself put on clean white t-shirts. Take two training knives (preferably soft rubber or an equivalent) and smudge lipstick along the edges and tips of both knives.

Someone yells "go" and you both attack each other—say for 30 seconds. Following the mêlée of slashes, hacks, thrusts and scrapes, pay close attention to what both your T-shirts look like. Add up the dashes and dots on both shirts and ask some down-to-earth questions if those were really razor sharp daggers instead of soft training toys: Who really won that bout? Would both of you have just walked away? Where did most of the punctures and slashes occur? Would it have been a survivable encounter? Now try this same drill with your partner coming at you with the lipstick-loaded training knife and you *without* a knife in your hand. This is a great reality check and should paint a vivid picture of personal combat with an edged weapon.

Mastery of handling any weapon comes only from dedicated years of discipline, strategy, timing, balance, footwork and efficient use of the weapon. However, one must first come to realize the gravity of what he may be getting himself into—in *any* personal combat scenario.

Part One—The Fundamentals of Edged Weapons Defense Technology

Back during the renaissance era, one could find a fencing school in almost any metropolitan city. This was true even up to as late as the early 19th century. However, with the advent of the semi-automatic pistol and advancements in firearms technology, the pistol took the place of the rapier and thus duels were fought with gunpowder as opposed to blades. So now when we want to go out and find a good school (or ANY school) that teaches the ancient secrets of self-defense versus an edged weapon attack, where would one go? The answer is the orient.

Such blade cultures as the Philippines, Malaysia, and Indonesia to this very day have preserved the teachings of their forefathers in a strict oral tradition. These ancient blade technologies were handed down from Grandfather to grandson, master to student and father to son in either the oral or dance-form tradition.

There are several books that have been written on this topic of the Filipino heritage which are fortunately available to those searching at this present day.

The meat and potatoes of what you will discover in the techniques and philosophies contained in this manuscript, reflects the essence of what has been passed down through the millennia to the modern masters of edged weapons such as Grandmaster Leovigildo Miguel Giron, Punong Guro Edgar G. Sulite, Master Antonio Diego, Master Rey Galang, Master Christopher Ricketts and Guro Dan Inosanto among others, on down to the author and now passed on to the reader.

What these great teachers have preserved and passed down to us is priceless information that was derived from the blood of battlefields and in some cases the unforgiving streets of Manila. What you're about to be presented is a portion of this technology as it is applied to modern self-defense against an edged weapon attack.

Choosing the Best

"What's the best blade out there?" and "How do I know what's the best knife for me?"

In the same way the ancient Greek philosopher Socrates answered his students' question with a question, the modern student of the blade must answer his questions with a question, "What exactly am I going to use the knife for?" Am I going to use my knife as a utility blade? Is it for self-defense? Is it for work? Perhaps it is a combination.

The Naked Edge: The Complete Guide to Edged Weapons Defense

You've probably heard the old saying "necessity is the mother of invention", well it happens to be especially true in the world of edge weapon application. A fisherman and a hunter need a different knife than a box-top opener who needs a different knife than a sushi chef who needs a different knife than a U.S. Navy SEAL. It's all a matter of application. Only after you've answered the question "What exactly am I going to use this knife for?"

There are two general classifications of blade type available today for the prospective buyer. These are known as—Fixed and Folding.

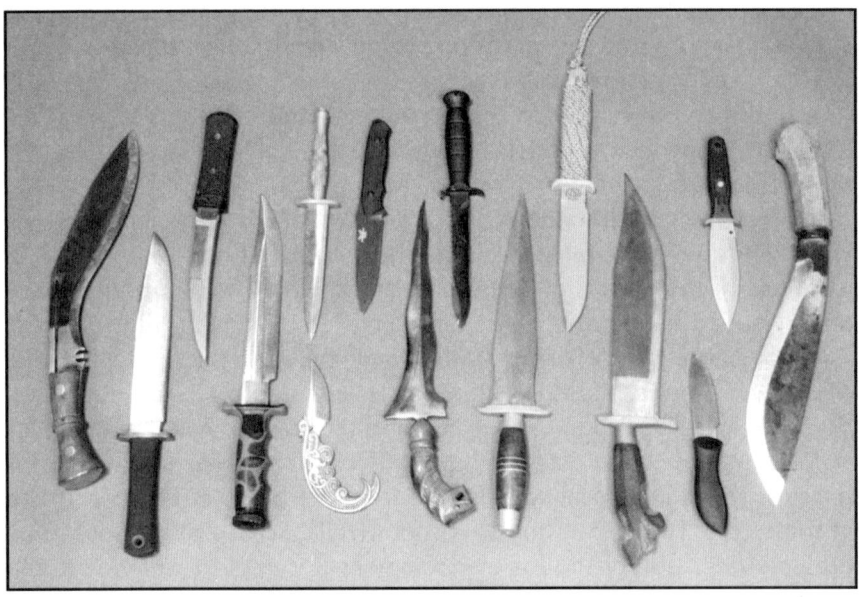

Here are some additional examples of fixed bladed knives. These weapons are most commonly carried in belt holsters.

A fixed blade can be defined as any pointed or sharp, single or double-edged blade secured to a fixed handle. Examples of a fixed blade would be the classic Bowie Knife, Scottish Dirk, K-Bar or the classic Rondel dagger.

Even a broken piece of glass or steel shank with duct tape wrapped around one end would classify as a fixed blade.

Part One—The Fundamentals of Edged Weapons Defense Technology

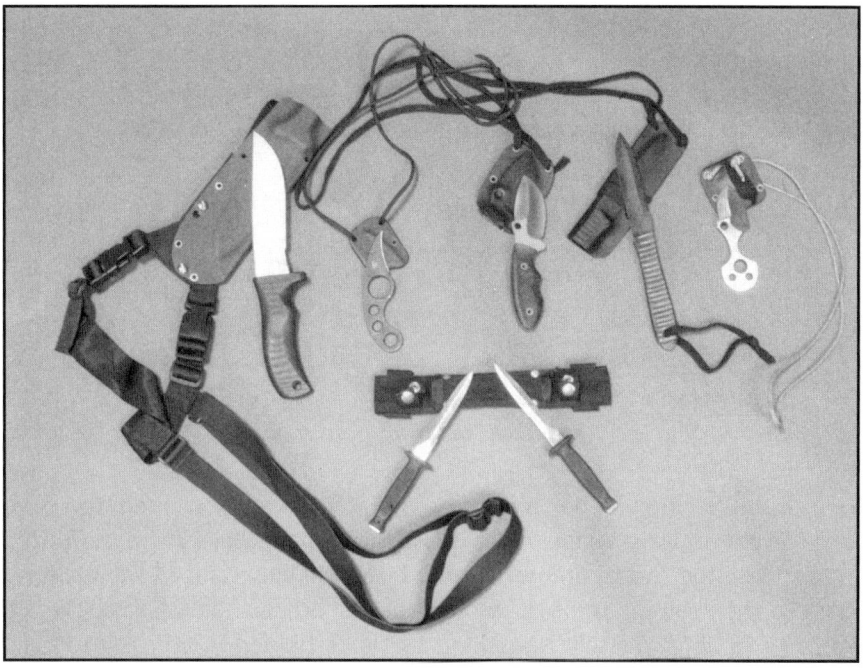

Neck knives and other draw systems.

A folding blade can be defined as any pointed or sharp, single or double-edged blade which in any way can be folded, coiled, bent or otherwise secured in such a fashion as to be rendered disabled in the "folded" position. Examples of a folding blade would be a pocketknife such as a Swiss Army or a combat folder. "Switch" blades and combat automatics also qualify as folding blades.

Folding blades can be further broken down into three identifying categories: 1. Mechanically operated 2. Gravity operated, and 3. Spring assisted or "Automatic."

If you're looking for a mechanically operated folding knife, a plethora of opening mechanisms is available for your selection. Some blades are enabled via manipulation of an opening mechanism using the thumb such as a hole, T-post, pin post, indents, groves or pocket catches. These types of mechanically operated folding knives are generally offered with spine or ridge-lock, liner-lock or bolt-lock securing systems.

Examples of various locking mechanisms such as the Liner lock, Ridge lock, and Bolt lock systems.

If you're looking for a gravity-operated knife, you generally have only a few options. Mainstream availability of the Balisong and Tri-fold make these the most common. Some historians have traced the Balisong back to the Philippines ("bali" which means "broken" and "soung' which means, "bone")—loosely translating to "knife hidden in a broken bone." As a result of overall appearance assumed in full operation, this knife is sometimes referred to as a "butterfly knife." Both the Balisong and Tri-fold are available in a multitude of different blade styles and lengths. Although technically referred to in various penal codes as "gravity-assisted" knives, these folders can be manipulated effectively only after many hours of dedicated practice.

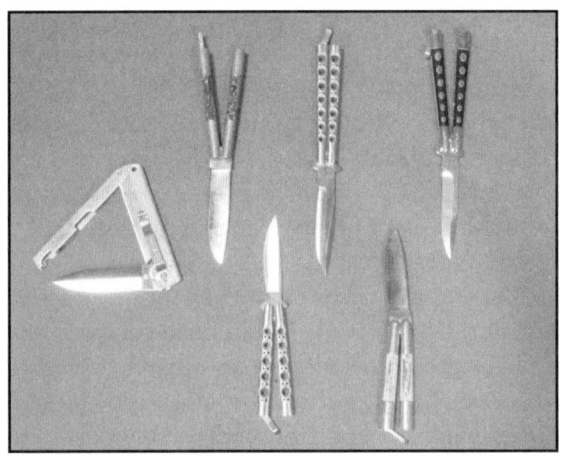

Examples of so-called "gravity-assisted" knives.

Part One—The Fundamentals of Edged Weapons Defense Technology

The third and final classification of modern folding blades is spring-assisted or "automatics." Due to the majority of state and federal laws governing the proliferation of edged weapons, there aren't too many of these types available to the general public. In certain states only law enforcement and military personnel are granted the right of ownership.

When choosing from the different types and styles of blades available on the market today, one must also consider two very important aspects of responsibility of blade ownership—legal and moral responsibility.

If you live in a state, which prohibits possession of a blade of any length greater than that of four inches, then your choice of fixed/ folder is limited to only those blade lengths that fall within the letter of the law. Likewise, if the law prohibits possession of any blade that is a specific type, say double edged, dirk or dagger, "switch" blade, etc., then you are again limited in your choices. You must also consider what type of carry system best suits your application. In some states it is against the law to carry a blade in your boot, hanging from your neck or hidden in your belt-buckle.

Moral responsibility is a subjective matter. However, to quote the training philosophy of one of today's top weapon instruction academies "It is incumbent upon those of us that carry weapons to be trained with those weapons and to keep our safety and skill levels as high as we possibly can."

Choosing what blade to carry is as personal as choosing what clothes to wear. It needs to fit your hand. It needs to fit your style. Above all, it needs to fit the answer to: "What exactly am I going to use this knife for?"

Training Knives

Today we have a tremendous variety of available training knives. With so many different shapes, sizes, materials, colors, styles and brands of training knives from which to chose—how do you know which is the best one to use?

There are training blades out there made from a selection of materials such as wood, plastic, rubber, resin, polymer, fiberglass, aluminum, PVC, Styrofoam, steel, brass, copper, ceramic and even leather (believe it or not). All these break down into four practical groups: wood, rubber, plastic and metal. There are advantages and disadvantages to each.

Wood is the cheapest. You can walk over to a tree, pull open your pocketknife and cut off a small branch. Take the piece of branch and whittle it down into the shape of a knife and your ready to go. Even easier is the next time you're in a hardware store drift past the wooden dowels and pick one up about six to eight inches in length and your ready to start training. The disadvantage is that if you really start whacking at your training partner let's say in sparring, wood is not very forgiving and you can end up bruising each other as well as experiencing the joy of splinters. Another small consideration is that a round wooden dowel-like shape is generally a little bit lighter and may not accurately emulate the knife you probably carry.

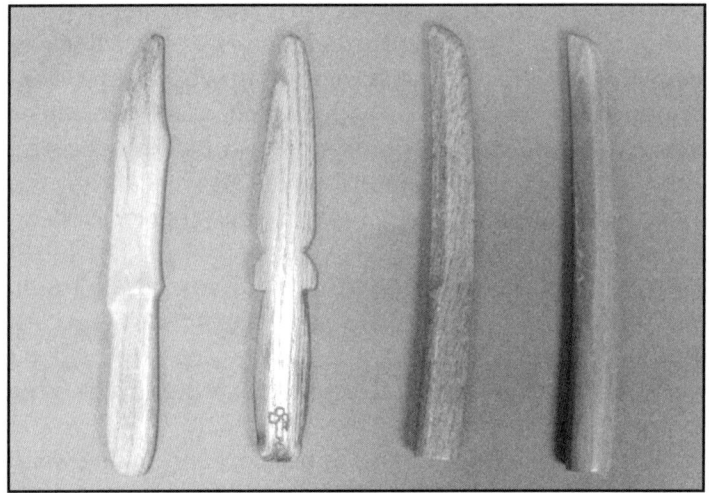

Custom examples of the classic wooden training knife.

Rubber is far more forgiving and is flexible just in case you get caught off guard with a solid incoming thrust. A good drill to try with flexible rubber training knives is to rub some chalk or even lipstick on both edges before you begin sparring (preferably wearing clean white t-shirts). One of the few disadvantages can be found during disarm training. The standard rubber training knife tends to bend quite easily and in most cases may not provide the rigidity necessary to execute realistic repetition during certain disarming techniques.

PART ONE—THE FUNDAMENTALS OF EDGED WEAPONS DEFENSE TECHNOLOGY

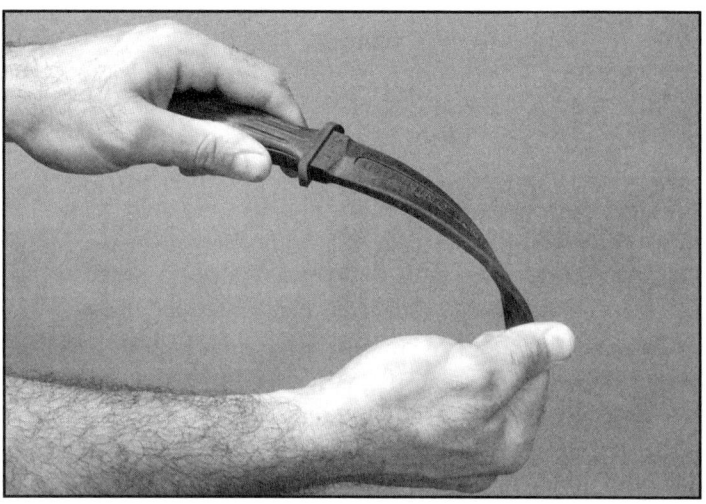

The typical rubber training knife.

Plastic and resin models are a bit more expensive, but much like wood (and unlike rubber) provide a sufficient rigidity to practice disarming techniques. Some of the better models I've seen to date are the fixed "Boot Knife" model produced by Sharkee, Inc. and the "Strider Trainer" by Strider Knives, Inc.—great training knives in my opinion.

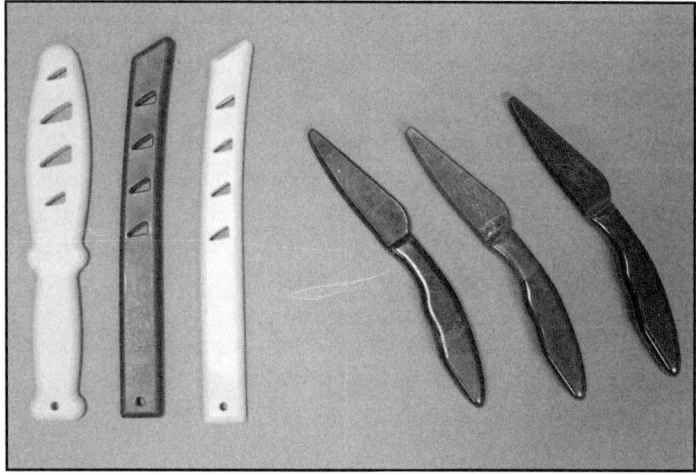

High-impact resin trainers made by Sharkee Inc. and Wobyrg Enterprises.

Metal training knives are by far the more expensive models. Although a bit more spendy, metal knifes more closely resemble actual knives in that they are made out of similar material and generally carry the same weight or "heft" as they say in the industry.

The human body goes through 160 biochemical changes when faced with a life and death situation. These changes are part of what is often called the fight or flight mechanism. Blood rushing to the legs for the purpose of fleeing causes one to grow light headed and faint. Blood rushing to the head and the flushing of the face are common in the fight response.

The primary biochemical changes, which negatively affect ones ability to respond, are an increased heart rate, tunnel vision and auditory exclusion. With this in mind it is essential that we train in such a manner as to excite the senses yet maintain safety. An aluminum training blade allows the practitioner to see the glimmer of the steel and feel the cold touch of its surface. These sensations are essential to attune the mind to the reality and results of improperly trained drills. One of the best selections of aluminum training knives (which I highly recommend) is from Edges2—superior workmanship at reasonable prices.

Examples of top of the line aluminum training blades by Edges 2.

PART ONE—THE FUNDAMENTALS OF EDGED WEAPONS DEFENSE TECHNOLOGY

Similar to wood and hard plastics, however, metal training knives can be quite unforgiving. Especially if you're sparring hard and fast with good training equipment such as training helmets, safety glasses and LAMECO training gear and your training partner tends to nail your body with maximum thrust and slashing power. You may want to consider a great sparring knife from a company called Sof-Stix which are custom designed for that type of hard play.

Some of the best hand and forearm protection I've run into over the years was created and produced by my late master Punong Guro Edgar G.

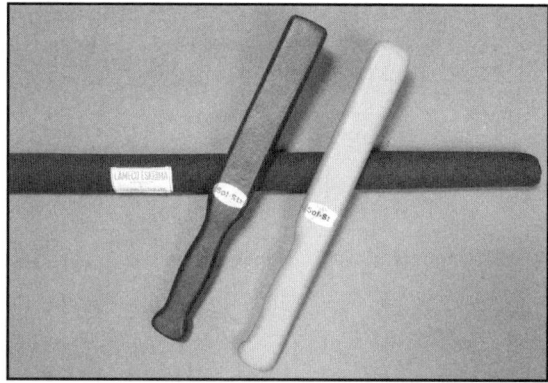

Safety gear and knives by Soft-Stix and LAMECO International.

Sulite, founder of LAMECO International. This combination of hand and forearm protection allows practitioners to strike at full speed using hard material training implements with little or no overall damage to the arm.

LAMECO Wrist Guard, Soft Training Stick and Forearm Guard

The very upper end of the training blades market for both realism and durability is the folding training knife. The advantage to these types of training knives is that they are generally the exact same shape, size and weight of your actual folding knife and can be carried and deployed in the exact same manner. This is a tremendous advantage for those who work carry and deployment drills. Two of the best I've seen to date are the new Spyderco Police Model Trainer and the Emerson Commander trainer—both of which I highly recommend to the serious student. These types of training blades additionally cut down on accidental hacking into your own flesh when practicing carry and deployment drills.

The same company who makes the actual knife also makes the most realistic training option. Here are two excellent examples by Spyderco and Emerson.

Safety, however, is the foremost consideration when you select a training knife. Yes, of course you want realism, but then again you have to go back to school or work the next day and you don't want to walk in with bandages or a patch covering the socket where your left eye used to be. Remember to use goggles and or protective head gear along with your training knives if you intend to do any sparring.

PART ONE—THE FUNDAMENTALS OF EDGED WEAPONS DEFENSE TECHNOLOGY

Basic Training Terminology

Centerline

Take your finger and draw an imaginary line from the middle of your forehead, over the tip of your nose, along your throat, across the middle of the sternum and to the groin. Your brain, eyes, lungs, throat, heart, liver, bladder, spleen and genitals are aligned either near or along this imaginary line commonly referred to by defensive tactics trainers across the globe as the CENTERLINE.

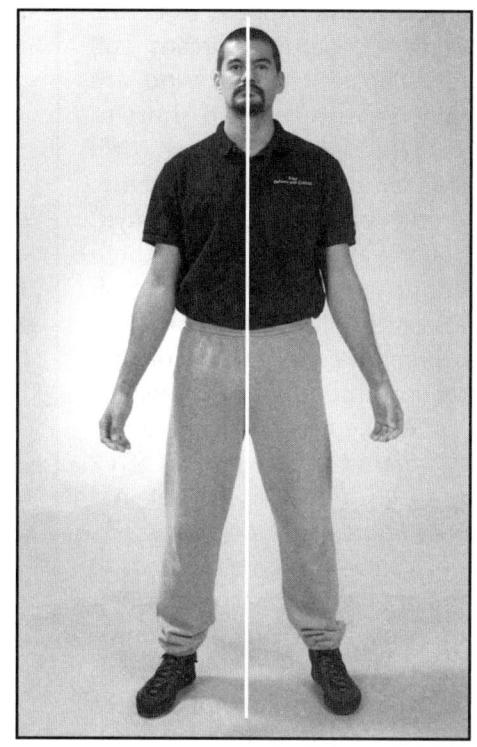

The Center Line.

The majority of the nine vital organs of the human body lay within the area of your CENTERLINE. Repeat, these are vital organs and you will want these around at the end of the day.

Let's take a run of the mill wild-eyed knife-wielding attacker coming at you with a razor sharp edge or knifepoint with every intention of running you all the way through. He doesn't want to clip your toenails or cut your hair—he wants your vitals. He wants to cut your throat or splay out your lower intestines or even stick you from behind in the kidneys. If any of these vital organs are punctured, lacerated or otherwise flayed by a sharp edge or point, then such a disruption could potentially render you either incapacitated or dead. This would cause considerable ramifications to your social calendar. Thus it is of primary importance to protect these vitals, which translates to protecting centerline.

Center Mass

CENTER MASS is a term referring to the majority area and heaviest part of the human body which is the torso (including the waistline). CENTER MASS is the primary target of any knife attack. It also happens to be the primary target for a firearm volley. Those students who are familiar with the two shots to CENTER MASS failure drill (Mozambique) know that the head is only a secondary target. Thus, as a primary target for both edged and ballistic weapon assaults—CENTER MASS must be a primary consideration of protection throughout the heat of battle. The hard and cold fact of the matter is that your CENTER MASS is a primary target in a knife fight.

What are some methods to protect center? One of the best options is to place distance between your vulnerable vitals and the ragged edge of a rusted shank. Simply facing your heels in the direction of the attack and competing for the best time possible against your high-school track team record for the 400meter dash can also accomplish this objective.

CENTER MASS as a primary target.

If the distance option isn't available to you, perhaps because you're stuck in a small alley or hallway, then place something like your car door, shovel, bag of groceries, lunch-box, umbrella, case of beer, a briefcase, your neighbor's dog, clothing or anything you can get your hands on between your center and harms way. Anything will do. This is a very easy yet effective counter-measure to exposing your innards to an incoming blade.

Granted, at first you may have slight reservations about sacrificing your expensive all-leather briefcase, favorite backpack or jacket by getting it slashed or stabbed. However, the consequences of accessory repair are far more palatable than having no protection of your CENTERLINE and getting run through like a stuck pig.

PART ONE—THE FUNDAMENTALS OF EDGED WEAPONS DEFENSE TECHNOLOGY

If the distance option isn't available to you, perhaps because you're stuck in a small alley or hallway, then place something like your car door, shovel, bag of groceries, lunch-box, umbrella, case of beer, a briefcase, clothing or anything you can get your hands on between your center and harms way.

The meat and potatoes to surviving any edged weapon encounter in the street boils down to only one simple concept. Regardless of where you may be or what you may be doing, be fully aware of your surroundings and more specifically what you can employ within your arms reach if you had to protect your CENTERLINE. The secret to protecting center is this—put something, anything (including lots of space) between that incoming edge or tip and your center.

Edged Weapon

An Edged Weapon can be defined as any material object fabricated out of metal, wood, plastic, glass, wire, or any other material capable of holding an edge or a point that can be used to lacerate or puncture human flesh. This can include, but is not limited to screwdrivers, broken glass, razor blades, sharpened belt buckles, folding knives, razor edge credit cards, syringes, prison shanks and kitchen knives.

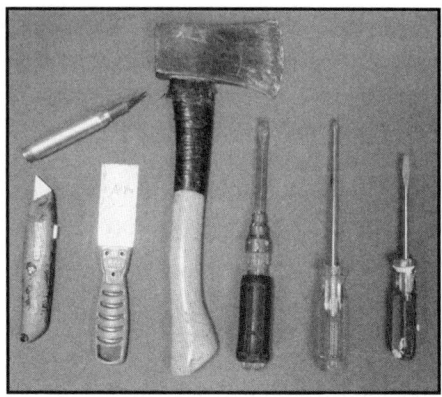

Various Edged weapons.

Safety Range

SAFETY RANGE is the subjective distance, which you (in defense of an edged weapon attack) consider a safe enough distance where you feel that your attacker wielding an edged weapon cannot get to you. Hand in hand with safety distance is SAFETY TIME.

Safety Time

SAFETY TIME is a subjective quantity of time relative to your safety. What that means is simply the further away from your attacker you end up—the more time it would take for him to get to you. Thus, if he were only a couple feet away from you (a very small safety distance) then your SAFETY TIME would only be a split second. If you had about a half a football field and three cars in between you and harm's way, now that's a much more comfortable amount of SAFETY TIME.

Contact Connection

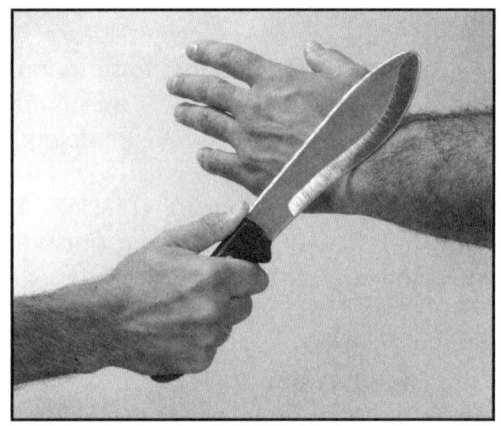

The CONTACT CONNECTION is the connection of your attacker to his knife and his knife to any part of your body.

The CONTACT CONNECTION is perhaps the single most important aspect of any edged weapon encounter. The CONTACT CONNECTION is the connection of your attacker to his knife and his knife to any part of your body. That is the deadly circuit, which must be avoided at all costs.

If your attacker has a knife connected to his hand and he's just waving it around and there's no connection or potential connection to your body, then you cannot be affected by something that is not in contact with your body.

The knife is a contact weapon. That means that in order for it to do what it does best, there must be contact between the edge or tip and your body. Thus, if the knife is attached to the hand of an attacker and his knife makes contact to any part of your body—then you've got what's called a CONTACT CONNECTION.

PART ONE—THE FUNDAMENTALS OF EDGED WEAPONS DEFENSE TECHNOLOGY

The ultimate objective in any edged weapon encounter is to avoid and control the CONTACT CONNECTION at any price.

Frozen Foot Syndrome

An interesting phenomenon that often occurs in an edged weapon attack scenario is what is known as "Frozen Foot Syndrome." This is where, we as humans are going about our day-to-day business and then all of a sudden—wham—a loud and unexpected crash or noise that scares the pants off your neighbor and guess what happens. Take a look at your body. Your fingers open, your weight lowers your chin pops up, your knees bend slightly and guess what—your feet are both cemented flat to the ground—frozen. This is an innate primal reaction, which occurs in most humans. Given that our first instinct is usually not a double spinning flying back kick to the head, it's important to ingrain reflexive responses that will engage even from a frozen foot posture.

Anatomy of Attack and Defense

The meat and potatoes of the anatomy of attack and defense can be described in a single word. That single word is control. Simply put, the winner is always the one is in most control what's going on in an altercation.

It is essential in an edged weapon altercation, to control three key factors. These important factors are control of position, control of distance and control of target size. These are the *structural* elements of any contact weapon encounter.

Let's take a look at each of these structural elements in detail.

SURVIVING AN EDGED WEAPON ALTERCATION

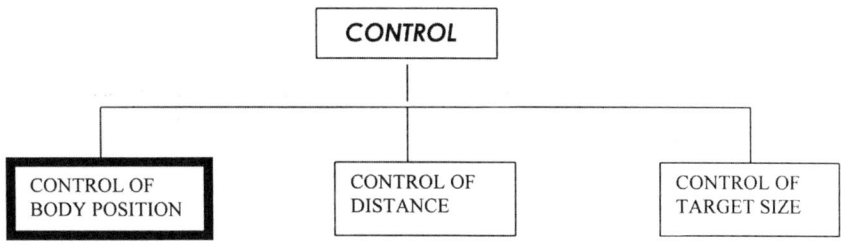

Before we get into the actual skills and drills to develop movement to superior position, it is important to understand the advantages and disadvantages of body position in relation to engagement against an edged weapon at close quarters. The three basic areas are the Inside Position, the Online Position, and the Outside Position.

CONTROL OF BODY POSITION
a. Move to superior position
b. Gain outside position advantage
c. Gain control of what's behind your target

Three Positions
a. Inside
b. On-line
c. Outside

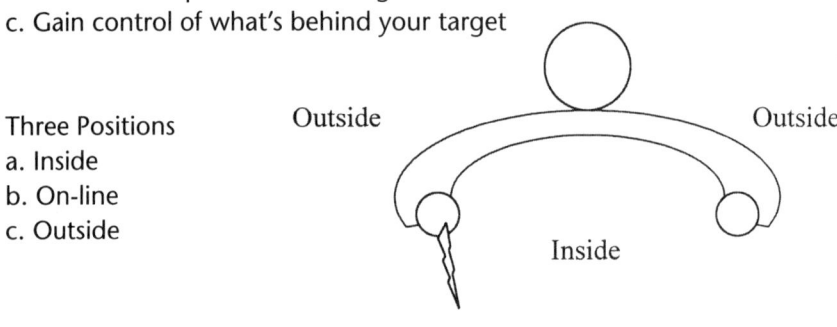

Online of Attack

The INSIDE position is where you find yourself in that area facing your opponent where you end up between both of his arms. The disadvantage of this position is that he has access to you at CONTACT RANGE with both his knives, opposite hand, elbows, knees, both feet and possibly a head butt.

The inside position of engagement.

Part One—The Fundamentals of Edged Weapons Defense Technology

The ON-LINE position is where you find yourself in that area facing your opponent where you end up aligned directly in front of his attacking weapon including his striking hands and/or striking feet. The disadvantage of this position is that he has immediate access to you at CONTACT RANGE with his knife or forward aggressive movement. The advantage is that you are not exposed to as potential a threat from his opposite hand, elbows, knees, both feet and possibly a head butt.

The on line position of engagement.

The OUTSIDE position is where you find yourself in that area facing your opponent where you end up directly on the outside of his attacking weapon including his striking hands and/or striking feet. The advantage of this position is that he has no immediate access to you at CONTACT RANGE with his knife or forward aggressive movement. Additionally you are not exposed to as potential a threat from his opposite hand, elbows, knees, both feet and possibly a head butt. There are no disadvantages to this position and is the best to end up if ever you find yourself in a self-defense situation.

One other distinct advantage of this position is that your moving around on the outside forces him to follow your movement. It is always the case that reaction is always slower than action. Thus you end up taking control of any situation at that point where you take control of the outside and force his reactions to your actions. This concept is quite similar to that of a boxer using ring generalship to

The outside position of engagement.

control the center of the ring and thus attempt to control the fight.

An interesting observation about the outside position, especially with regards to edged weapon defense is that if you look down on the body from above more than 75% of positional area belongs to the outside. The trick is to deftly maneuver from the INSIDE position past the ON-LINE position to get to all that open area on the OUTSIDE.

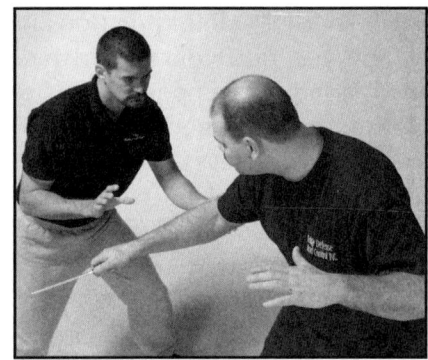

More than 75% of positional area belongs to the outside.

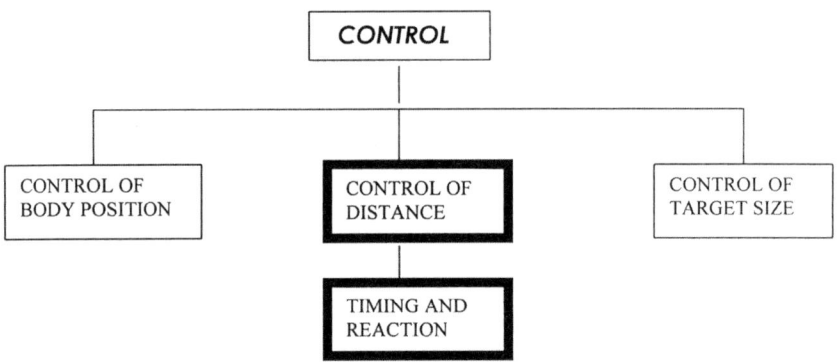

Distance, Timing, and Reaction

The three most important *skill* elements of an edged weapons encounter are distance, timing and reaction. These three skill elements work together like gears in a motor to produce the best possible reaction to the action of an attack. One who has developed the important skills of controlling distance, understanding timing and quickening reaction, has a far greater chance of surviving an edged weapon attack than one who does not.

PART ONE—THE FUNDAMENTALS OF EDGED WEAPONS DEFENSE TECHNOLOGY

The most important of these three is distance. Whether you're trying to hit a bull's eye by throwing darts or making a shot with a basketball or even tossing a piece of crumpled paper into a wastebasket, the ability to gauge distance by feel or sense is an absolute necessity. How much more difficult does your job get if your target is moving? Now imagine that your target can cut, slash, hack or even puncture you—this really makes the job a nightmare.

The best range to be at in a knife fight is about 1,200 yards away looking at your opponent through modern optics mounted on a high-powered rifle. Of course, most of us don't have this opportunity in our daily lives. For those of us who don't, it becomes a necessity to understand which response will work for you and at which distance.

The basic distances at conversational range for any edged weapon encounter can be divided into three simple ranges. These are—non-contact range, contact range and extreme close quarters range or ECQ.

Non-contact range is defined as that distance where both the attacker and the defender are just outside of mutual arm's-length reach.

 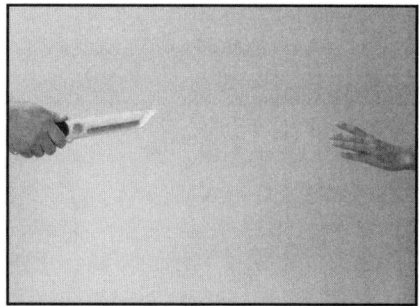

*Training Partner B and Training Partner A (with knife)
face each other at non-contact range.*

Contact range is defined as that distance where both the attacker and the defender can touch wrist to wrist if they both held there arms outstretched. Some Filipino knife fighting (Kali/ Eskrima/ Arnis) systems commonly refer to this range as pulso y pulso.

The Naked Edge: The Complete Guide to Edged Weapons Defense

 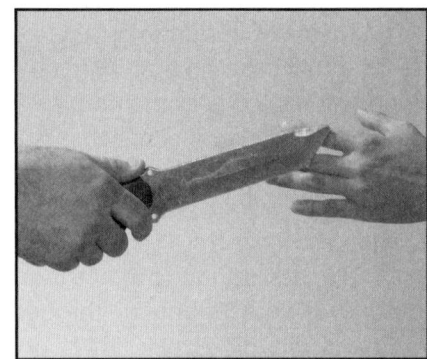

Training Partner B and Training Partner A (with knife) face each other at contact range.

Extreme Close Quarters or ECQ is defined as that distance where both the attacker and the defender can access a vital area of the body by simply extending their arms. Certain edge weapons trainers, law enforcement academies and military training schools also refer to this as Close Quarter Combat (CQC) range.

 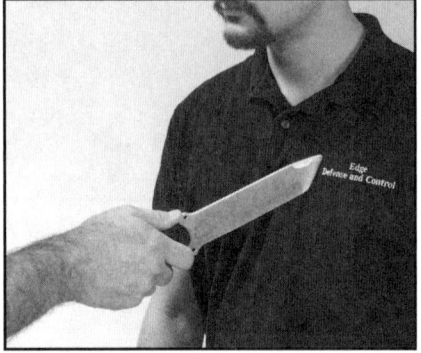

Training Partner B and Training Partner A (with knife) face each other at extreme close quarters (ECQ) range.

Part One—The Fundamentals of Edged Weapons Defense Technology

As painfully apparent as it may seem, this point really needs to emphasized: The further you are away from the edge and tip of that attacking blade, the more time you have to get away. This is the most important knife defensive tactic axiom in the book—*distance buys you time.*

There is, however, a time and a place when you must "go in." These are the times when you simply cannot gain distance (especially at ECQ range). I will address this in greater detail later.

Control of Distance
  Identify the contact connection
  Break the contact connection
  Make the decision to "Get in" or "Get out"

Much like cars traveling on the freeway, the further away you are from your destination, the longer it takes to reach that destination. This same rule of thumb can be applied in a knife fight. The further you are away from the incoming edged or tip, the more time you have to completely disengage.

The closer you get, the less time you have to react. This is the definition of a car accident. If you have plenty of time to see the guy blow through a red light, then you have lots of time to react. But the less distance you have, the less time you have to react. There is a direct proportional relationship between time and distance. This is known as the time-distance variable.

At non-contact range, the best technique to use is footwork. Especially if you are unarmed and have nothing to place between yourself and your attacker. Again, the absolute best thing to place between you and your attacker at this range is distance. By using your footwork you create more distance and can thus achieve your ultimate goal in any edged weapons encounter—get out of there as fast as you can. You don't want to risk changing your distance to a closer range (which gives you less time to react) and have to reckon with a razor sharp blade—odds are NOT in your favor and you WILL GET CUT.

If you get caught at contact range, again your best option is to use your feet and create distance as quickly as possible. However, you may not be able to move quickly enough and thus may require the use of your hands or elbows. At contact range you may need to employ a downward or upward deflection in addition to footwork to escape. Remember you have increased your odds on being cut at this range and have simultaneously decreased your reaction time.

The ugliest range of them all is extreme close quarters (ECQ). Here, you are at maximum risk of getting cut open like a ripe cantaloupe and decreasing your reaction time to almost nothing. Best is to use your shirt or briefcase or a shopping bag or whatever you have in your hands to place a barrier between yourself and the edge/ tip of that incoming blade. You may have only your elbows. This gives you the split second you need to move from ECQ to contact range and then to non-contact range and eventually completely out of range.

In any event and at any range, we are reminded by the ancient master as well as the modern weapons instructor: what was true for the powerful legions of ancient Rome is still true for you caught in an edged weapons encounter today– *distance is your friend.*

Getting in or Getting Out
Although distance is your friend and the best place to be in an edged weapon attack is to the outside and at non-contact range, or even better—completely out of range, there are certain situations that exist which make it literally impossible to change ranges, use footwork or even attempt any hand techniques in order to break the contact connection. This is your worst nightmare scenario. The very best you could hope for would be to at least *control* the contact connection. These are the absolute worse case conditions you could possibly experience.

You could be pinned in by a rear obstruction negating any footwork. You could be up against somebody so close and so fast that you can't even execute hand techniques. Although not very pretty, there are various solutions to these ugly problems and I will cover these in greater detail later in this book.

Mobility

If someone pulls out a knife and is moving toward you there are a couple of factors that require analysis. As mentioned earlier, if you freeze frame the attack and draw a line from the tip/ edge of the attacker's weapon to your CENTERLINE (imaginary line drawn from your forehead to your groin), we can call this the *line of attack* or LOA.

Part One—The Fundamentals of Edged Weapons Defense Technology

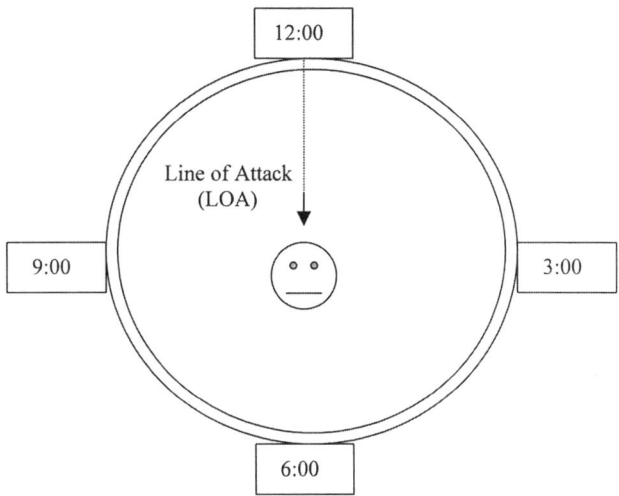

Imagine you are standing on the face of a clock. If he is at 12:00 and you are in the middle of the face, then he is directly in front of you. No matter what position the attacker may move to on the clock face, you can still connect a line from his weapon to your CENTERLINE and call this the line of attack (LOA). The laws of physics hold that after he commits to a slash or thrust or some other type of attacking motion with the knife, he *must* follow along that same LOA to reach his intended target. Your response is to step off that line of attack as quickly as possible to reduce his chances of connecting.

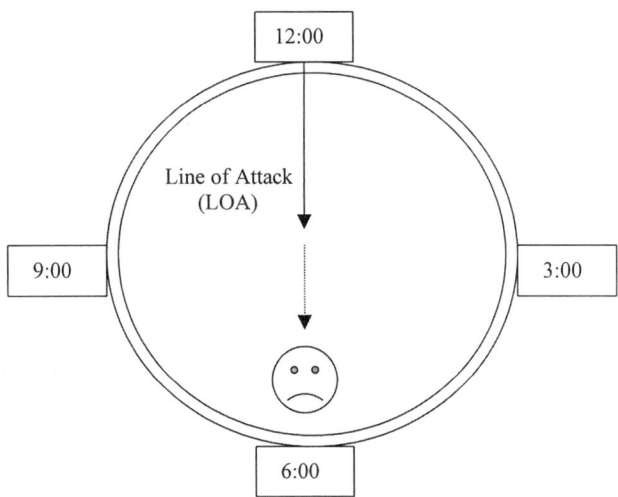

Using our clock face scenario above, he attacks from the 12:00 position. Now, if your standing in the middle of the clock and you take one step straight back then you're still along the same LOA and it's just a matter of time before he closes the gap and hits his target as a guy running forward will always outrun a guy running backwards

The ancient masters have figured out that the best way to step off the line of attack is to step out 45 degrees either forward or backward from the attack.

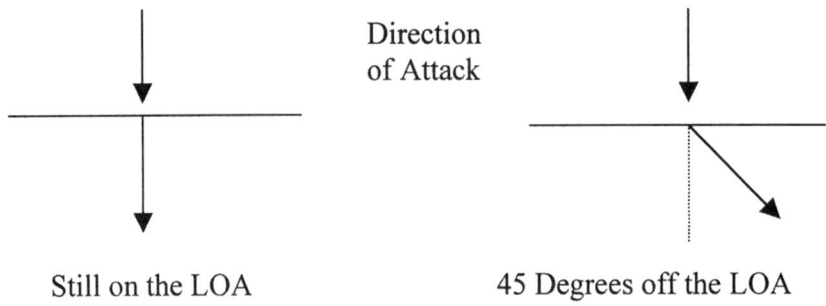

Still on the LOA   45 Degrees off the LOA

If you were to step off 45 degrees back, say to 4:00 O'clock, then this would force him to change his direction and motion in order to pick up the new line of attack.

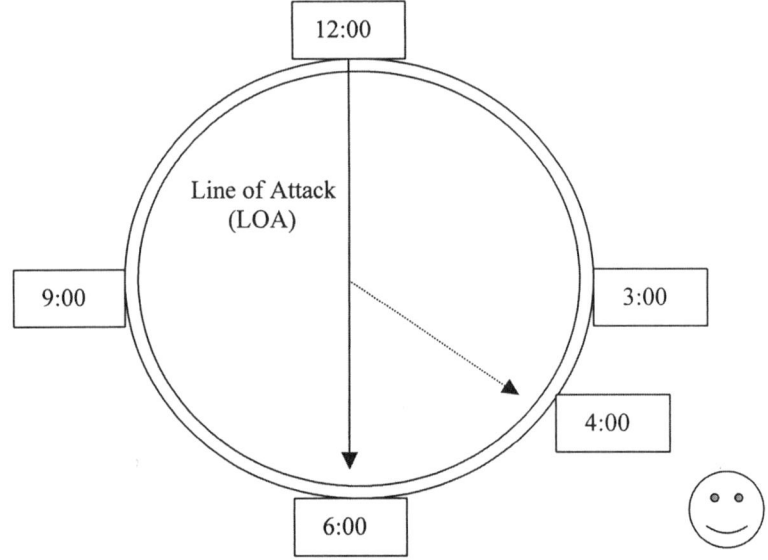

Part One—The Fundamentals of Edged Weapons Defense Technology

In other words, the closer you stay to the LOA, the better his chances are in hitting his target. The faster you move off that LOA (using 45 degree angles) the less chance he has of hitting his target and the more time you gain to further react.

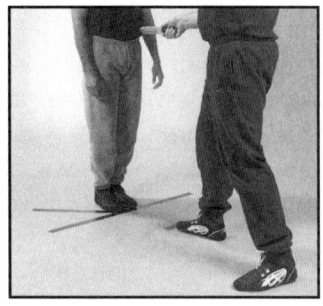 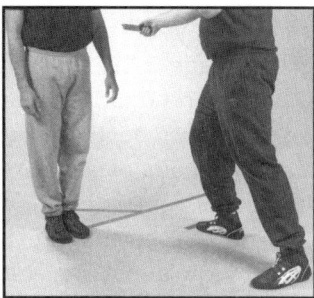 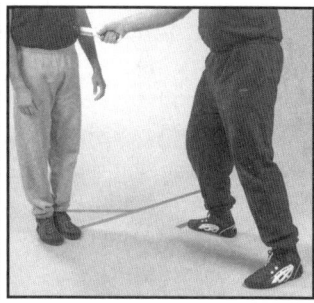

By stepping laterally, you may have evaded the initial contact connection; however, you are still well within range of the arc of attack and are still reacting to his actions.

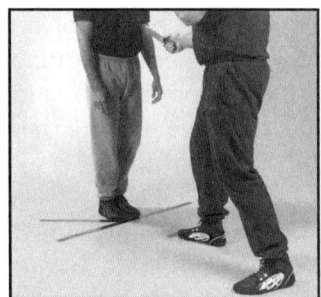  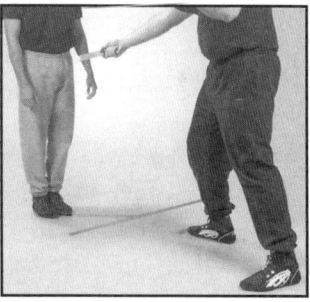

By exerting the exact same amount of effort (a single step) but this time on a 45-degree angle, you have not only defeated the primary contact connection but have accomplished two rather important objectives: 1. You are now off the line of attack and out of range for his next strike. 2. It is now you who has gained the advantage of taking action and now he must react to your movement.

Carry and Deployment

The two most important primary functions of self-defense with an edged weapon are how to carry the knife and how to deploy it.

How can you carry a knife? Well, the real answer is any way that you can think of. However, there are certain advantages and disadvantages to each method. For example, if you have a fixed blade dagger and carry it as a neck-knife. The advantage is that it is concealed and most people won't suspect a neck knife. The disadvantage is that, unless you wear it over your shirt or jacket (which defeats the concealment advantage), you must first pull up your shirt and/ or jacket to access the handle, pull it from it's sheath and then assume a fighting posture—all of this takes time. Advantage is that it's convenient, provides the element of surprise and easy access. Disadvantage is that it's legality may be questionable in certain jurisdictions and that it may take a little more time to access especially if you're wearing a t-shirt, sweatshirt, sweater, heavy jacket and a scarf in the middle of winter in Detroit, Michigan.

Another type of carry is the classic side pocket carry. The classic combat folder clip-on can easily be carried in either of the side pockets, back pockets, behind or on the belt in front (cross-draw), behind or on the belt in back, in the shirt collar and if the knife is small enough inside the actual shirt pocket. The advantage to this carry is convenience and legality. The disadvantage is that it may turn out to be a two or three step process to access the folded unit, flip open the blade and acquire a combat grip on the handle.

Another method of carry is what is called the "Dundee Rig" (named after an Australian character in a popular movie), which allows instant access to a rather large blade with one simple motion. Advantage is that it's a very large blade and instant access. Disadvantage is that its legality may be questionable in certain jurisdictions and uncomfortable to wear during lengthy business meetings.

As far as carrying a knife or dagger, the very best is just to have it already in your hand. Of course, other people may find this method of carry quite offensive and in most cases you will be questioned by local law enforcement as to *why* you are carrying a knife in your hand. The second best is a fixed blade located in a sheath external to any clothing such as an exposed side sheath or boot sheath as this makes for instant access, but may have questionable legal ramifications depending upon where you live. The most practical in our society today is the carry and deployment of the modern high-tech combat folder.

Part One—The Fundamentals of Edged Weapons Defense Technology

Deployment simply means pulling it out and acquiring a combat-ready posture. The best method of deployment is to secure a good solid grip on the handle from its place of carry and all the way through deployment and operation.

Three really good reasons why corrections, security and law enforcement personnel should become familiar with the study of carry and deployment.

Certain weapons instructors in the defensive tactics training industry (including myself) refer to the act of deploying a weapon as a "presentation." In the example of a fixed carry and deployment the presentation is simple. You just grab the handle and pull it out of its sheath and there you are with a point between you and the threat with a smile on your face.

In the example of a combat folder, there are just a couple more steps. 1. Secure a firm grip on the handle. 2. Pull the weapon from its carry location, 3. Using either one or two hands, unfold and lock the blade into its operational position and 4. Assume an effective combative posture.

All four of these above steps must be practiced many times to ensure proficiency when you need it most. You can practice while watching TV, or on the phone, or while stuck in traffic or just before you go to bed at night. The magic secret to deployment is *practice*. Number of times executed is equal to degree of certainty when it really matters.

One word of wisdom with regards to carry—*always carry your knife in the same place*. Because if you need it in a hurry you don't want to have to add the very slow step of thinking, "where did I put my knife?" Imagine getting into your car in the morning and every day someone changed the position of your break, clutch and gas pedal. Sure you'd figure it out after a while, but in an emergency you'd better know where the break is. Same way with your knife once you decide on a carry position that fits your personal profile—*don't change it!*

In our modern politically correct oriented society (especially in the Peoples Republic of California), it's almost a crime to defend yourself either with or without a knife (and in some places even with your bare hands). However, if you chose the advantage of carry and deployment of an edged weapon, and support that choice with training in safety and operation, you must first check with local law enforcement to ensure that your method of carry is within the confines of the law for your area.

Carry Positions

Once you've selected the knife of your choice, now you must decide where to carry it. Barring the neck, boot and other questionable carry positions, the most commonly accepted by most states in the union are plain view carries. Most laws ascertain that knife must be in "plain view" and not "concealed"—which is an arbitrary term and generally subjected to the discretion of an arresting officer. Now that you've selected the knife you wish to carry, the next question is where can you carry a folding knife and how do you get it out (deploy) from the carry position?

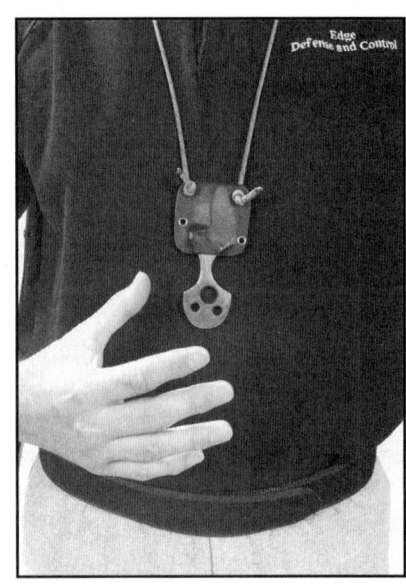

Neck Carry.

There are eight basic positions that a folding knife may be carried. Six are considered same side carry and two cross body carry.

Part One—The Fundamentals of Edged Weapons Defense Technology

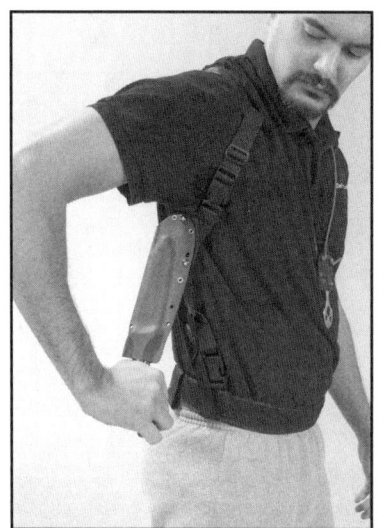 

Under arm carry.

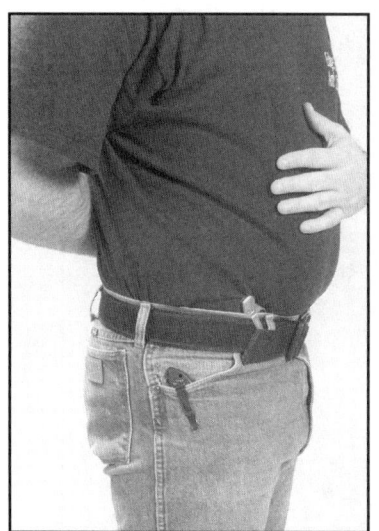

*Same Side Carry Positions:
1—right waistband,
2—right pocket.*

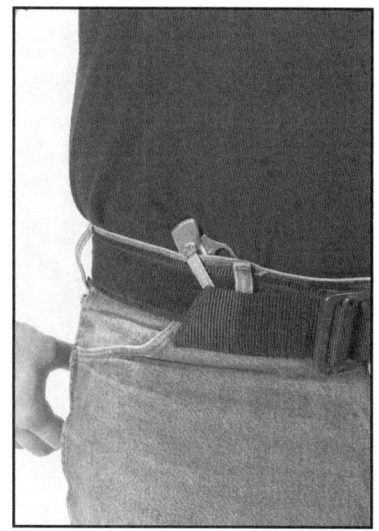

Right waistband or hip carry.

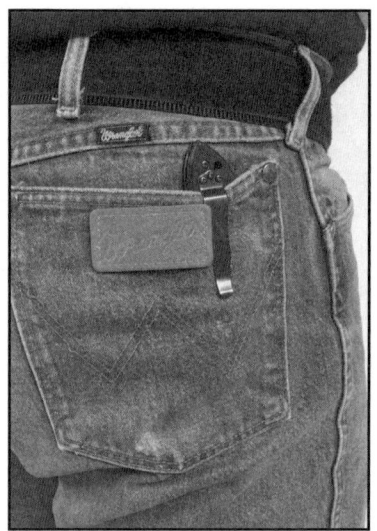

Rear Pocket Carry.

 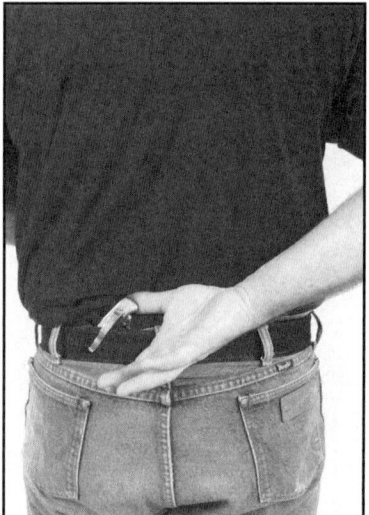

Cross Body Carry Positions: 1—front waistband, 2—rear waist band.

Closing Your Folding Knife

Remember, safety is always first. The number one safety rule is never point a knife or its edge at anything you're not willing to cut or puncture. This includes your own body. The procedure for properly closing your knife is as follows. First, position thumb on closing mechanism and engage closing mechanism. Then, gently push blade slightly past open position. Remove fingers from path of the blade's incoming edge and point. Turn the edge and tip away from your body and reposition your closing hand without losing contact with the back of the blade again carefully avoiding edge and tip. Lightly push on back of blade close to the hinge until closed, remove closing hand and return the folder to your carry position.

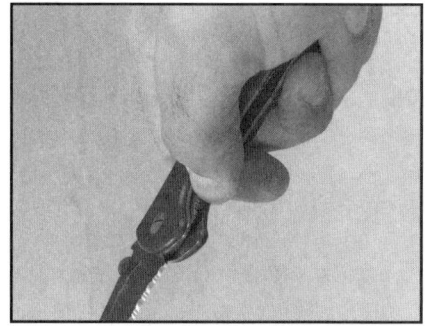

Position thumb on closing mechanism and engage closing mechanism.

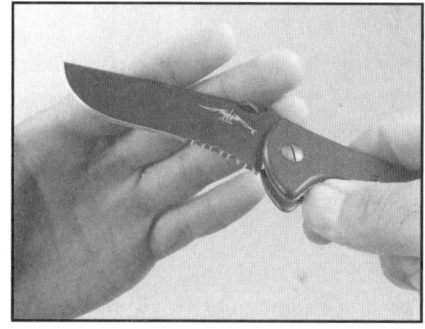

Gently push blade slightly past open position.

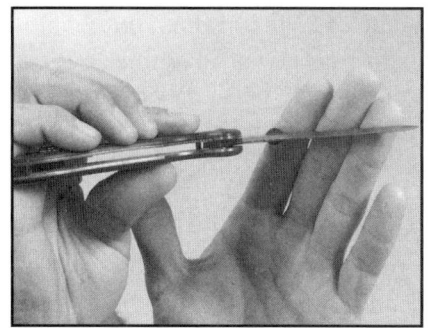

Remove fingers from path of the blade's incoming edge and point.

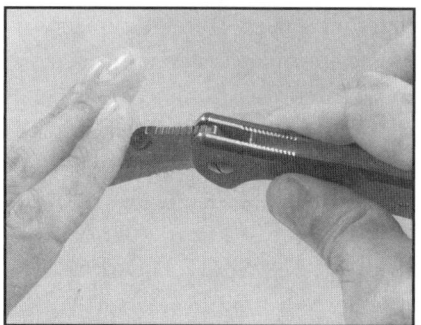

Turn the edge and tip away from your body and reposition your closing hand without losing contact with the back of the blade, again carefully avoiding edge and tip.

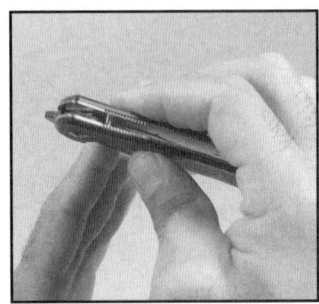 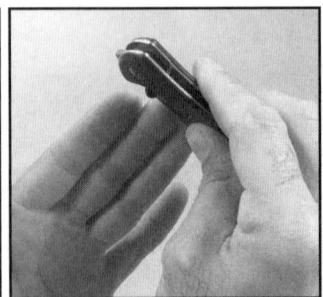 

Lightly push on back of blade close to the hinge until closed, remove closing hand and return the folder to your carry position.

Grips

One of the most frequently asked questions about handling a knife is "What's the best way to hold a knife?" This is just about the same as someone asking you "What's the best way to open a door?" There are many different ways to open a door. It is simply a matter of what kind of door it is that you want to open. For example, if the door has a doorknob on it, then you must first turn the doorknob and then open the door. If it's the kind of door that has a bar going across, then you simply grab the bar and then open the door. With this configuration you would then need to figure out if it's a pushing or pulling action.

Just as there are many types of handles and opening actions on different doors, so are there many types of handles and opening actions on different knives. Depending upon what type of knife it is that you're holding, determines how you are going to handle it. For example, if it's a modern combat folding knife (such as a liner-lock, bolt-lock or ridge-lock style), then the handle will tend to be very narrow and come with both a forefinger stop and some type of thumb rest. In this case, you would use a saber grip to take advantage of the design features. However, if the knife happens to be a fixed blade, where the handle is much thicker, such as the K-Bar, Scottish Dirk or Bowie, then perhaps a hammer grip or reverse grip may better suit your application. In simplified terms, *design determines grip.*

However, regardless of design, there are two key elements that forge a rock solid grip. These are:
1. Creating friction
2. Locking the wrist.

PART ONE—THE FUNDAMENTALS OF EDGED WEAPONS DEFENSE TECHNOLOGY

Creating Friction is literally producing enough friction where the handle of the knife is molecularly bonded to the skin of your hand. Have you ever walked across a room holding something in your hand and then accidentally bumped into something with your hand? The impact immediately loosened your grip and most likely, whatever you were holding fell from your grasp. The same principle applies to gripping a knife. If you've ever really stabbed a piece of wood or thrust into a training tire, then you know how much pressure is applied against your grip at point of impact. The last thing you want, when it really matters, is to have your knife blasted away from your hand as the result of a weak grip.

There are four points of contact that create enough friction to establish a "secured grip." These are considered primary points of contact and are:
1. Thumb
2. Forefinger
3. Pinky finger
4. Surface of the palm.

Try this experiment. Grab your combat folder, open the blade and hold it in your hand.
1. Take your thumb, place it on the thumb rest (located at the foremost position of the spine at the base of the blade).
2. Place your forefinger securely on the finger rest (located opposite the thumb rest).
3. Wrap your pinky finger tightly around the base (butt of the knife).
4. Squeeze the handle with the remaining fingers so as to eliminate any space between the flat side of the handle and the surface of your palm. What you now have in your hand is a secured grip.

With your secured grip, wiggle the knife around in the air. Now, lift your thumb off and wiggle it around. Does it feel different? OK, put your thumb back on and take off your forefinger and do the same thing. Now try it with the pinky. Finally, create a gap between the surface of the handle and the surface of your palm. What is the difference in handling with less friction? The more friction you can create the more solid your grip.

Locking the wrist is the second key element of establishing a secured grip. The Japanese have a term "kamai" which, when training with the Yoroi Toshi, Wakazashi or Katana is applied to the wrist. Sometimes referred to as "Kamai Wrist", the alignment of the first two knuckles of the weapon hand with the base of the wrist joint, locks the bones of the hands, wrist and forearm in a natural alignment. This locking of the wrist combined with your secured grip gives you the best way to hold a knife—especially when you really need it.

Next question, now that you've established a secured grip, how do you determine the use of your grip when operating the edge?

One of the greatest recorded fencing masters of antiquity (both rapier and dagger) was a Master Instructor named Giacomo Di Grassi who lived during the Elizabethan era. His famous book *His True Arte of Defence* (published in 1594) is one of only the oldest training manuals on knife and swordplay surviving. In it, the master describes how a wrist cut is quick but not so strong, while the force generated from the shoulder is much stronger but not so quick. The edged weapon fighter must be trained to always have at his disposal, the balance of the two.

Therefore, when delivering a slash or thrust, the Master recommends "he shall only use the compass of the elbow and the wrist: which as they be most swift, so are they strong enough, if they be orderly handled."

Even the blade masters of antiquity stressed the practical importance of employing a secured grip in an edged weapon encounter.

In a self-defense situation you should be able to both hold your knife and at the same time identify the way an attacker may be gripping his knife. It's important to identify what's coming at you so that you can react properly to the threat. Similar to approaching a yellow light—you either slow down or accelerate based on your position. The key being where you are and what color the light is. The same thing applies to grip—recognized what can be used and at what range—we'll get into this a little bit later.

We are limited to the confines of the human anatomy in that the tip can only point in either of two directions (up or down) and the thumb can only be placed in either of two positions (on the fingers or on the knife handle). Thus, there are several grips possible using these combinations of positions but for purposes of our study we'll only address the four most effective and most commonly found and used in modern times. These grips are known as the Hammer Grip (holding the handle as if you were holding a hammer and driving a nail into the wall), the Saber Grip (as if you were holding a modern fencing saber), the Slashers Grip (thumb on fingers), and the Ice Pick Grip (thumb on handle). In the Filipino martial arts they are sometimes refered to as Tusok, Sak Sak, Langit, Lupa, and Pakal (depending upon what dialect you speak).

Part One—The Fundamentals of Edged Weapons Defense Technology

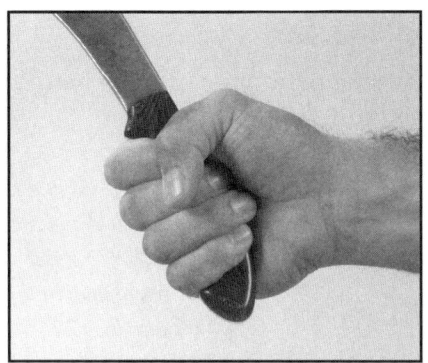

The Hammer Grip.

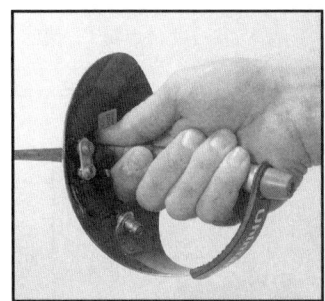 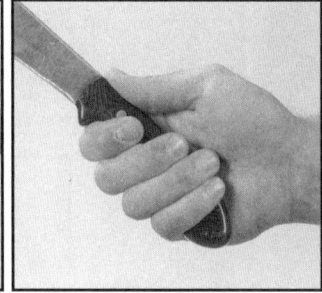 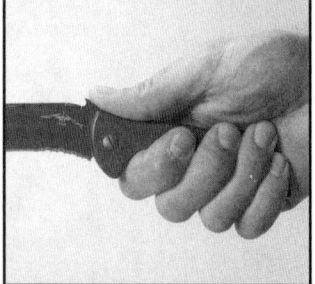

The Saber Grip.

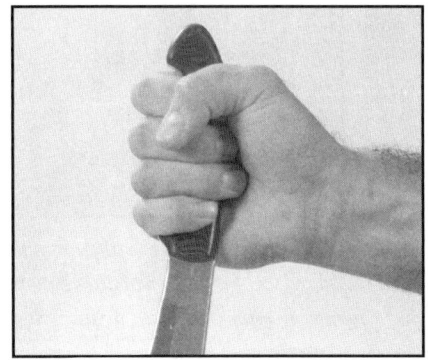 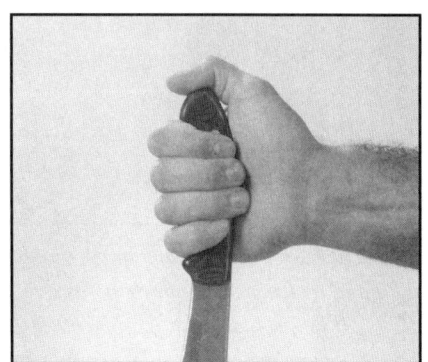

The Reverse Grip.   *The Ice Pick Grip.*

Edged Weapon Attacks

Three of the most common types of edge weapon attacks are the slash, the hack and the thrust.

The slash is defined as a full-follow-through forehand or backhand motion. Much like a stroke in tennis or golf, the slash is a full follow-through motion that covers an arc of attack usually wide enough to protect your entire centerline. If you would, visualize a baseball bat cracking a home run with a full swing and follow-through; this is an example of the slash.

The hack is defined as a quick backhand and return or quick forehand and return. If you would, visualize a baseball bat swung really hard into a trampoline and it bouncing back from point of impact to the exact same position it started; this is an example of a hack.

The thrust is simply defined as any forward stabbing or puncturing motion following either a curved or straight-line trajectory. This is a very common offensive maneuver and is often wrongfully omitted from defensive training.

Part One—The Fundamentals of Edged Weapons Defense Technology

A thrust most often attacks and returns to the same beginning posture but will pass by to a new posture if it misses. In motion it may be similar to a slash or a hack.

There are many more types of edged weapon attacks. However, for purposes of this particular manuscript we will limit our focus to these three.

Defensive Hand Postures

There are three basic hand postures that you must be proficient with before moving on. These are Palm up, Palm Down and Palm Vertical postures.

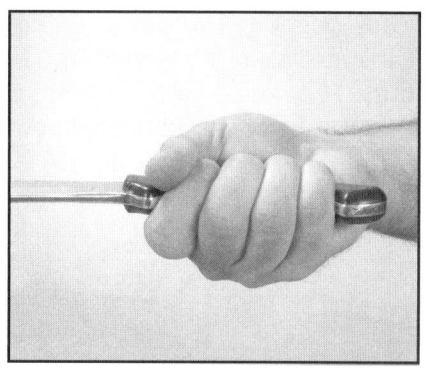

Knife in palm up posture.

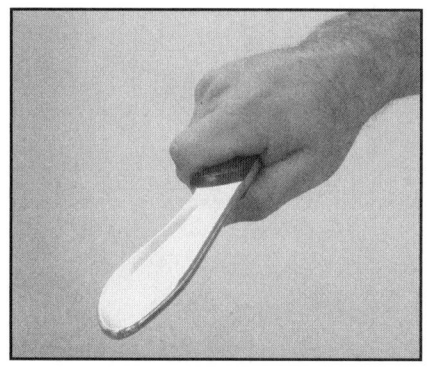

Knife in palm down posture.

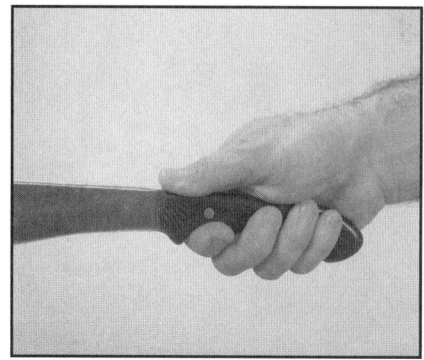

Knife in palm vertical posture.

The Naked Edge: The Complete Guide to Edged Weapons Defense

There are only so many positions in which to posture the knife hand. These are similar to the positions found in modern fencing. There are five basic positions. The first is High Open, the second is Low Open. The third is High Closed and the fourth is Low Closed. The last is center or Ready position. This posture is called Pasulong Dulo or tip towards the front in the Filipino martial arts. These postures can be practiced with all four of the previously listed knife grips.

High Open defensive posture.

Low Open defensive posture.

High Closed defensive posture.

PART ONE—THE FUNDAMENTALS OF EDGED WEAPONS DEFENSE TECHNOLOGY

Low Closed defensive posture.

Ready or Center posture.

Gross Motor Skills

Each individual talks, walks, eats, and fights in their own way. Like a suit of clothing techniques fit some individuals while they are not suited for the next persons particular body type, natural ability, or mind set. Guro Dan Inosanto said it best with the following advice. He said that "You must adjust to your personal strengths and innate abilities." However, just because a technique may feel awkward at first does not mean it should be discarded. It is often the case, like breaking in a new pair of boots, that the new technique and the body both need a little time with each other.

As my teacher, Guro Dan Inosanto says—"When playing baseball with a little kid and teaching him how to field grounders, you don't rip the ball into his head at 200 feet per second. You start off slowly and then gradually increase your speed and power up to the abilities of the individual. That is what you will need to do with your partner." Just like pulling out into an intersection—when the light turns green its time to go. Keep in mind that good timing is independent of speed so remember to train safely and gradually increase your speed to the abilities of your training partner and yourself.

Turn One Way

The first of our gross body motor skills, as with many others, we draw from natural movement. To create a defense on an unnatural or synthetic motion would take an extremely long time to bring up to combat speed. As an example, if some crazed fugitive waving around a rusted screwdriver is chasing you down from your office all the way to your car you will most likely not have time to warm up, stretch out, and perform the deadly-flying-monkey-jumping-eyebrow-block.

The first gross body skill is performed just like you're going to pick up your keys or something that you dropped onto the ground. This motion is called "bobbing." Timing is going to be the key in executing this movement but that will be covered later.

Keeping your hands up above your waistline turn both shoulders and look one way turning your lead shoulder downward as if going to pick up your dropped car keys from the deck.

Keeping your hands up now turn both shoulders the other way turning your lead shoulder downward as if you were going to pick your dropped car keys from the deck.

QuickShield™

Another Gross Motor Skill is QuickShield™. This defense will require you to posture your arms so that your elbows protrude like a helmet or an extension of your nose. The key to movements of this kind is that they must be easy to remember and capable of being executed by any individual who may need them. The key points to QuickShield™ are to keep

Part One—The Fundamentals of Edged Weapons Defense Technology

your chin tucked, cover your center, and remember to keep your palms facing inward. The steps are as follows.

Step one, tuck the chin into the shoulder.

Step two, move the elbows so as to cover your centerline.

Incorrect position. Notice face, neck and centerline exposed. Arms are held too low and away from centerline to be effective in defense if needed.

Correct position. Notice elbow in center, chin tucked, eyes on threat and second hand up high and near center.

Later on in the book we will combine the Turn One Way Movement with the QuickShield™ movement to produce an effective high line defense. Until then, focusing on the basic movement, it's important to execute the chin, move your elbow to center and engage your secondary hand all in one smooth motion. This ensures that your natural centerline shield will be there when you really need it.

One side note: be sure that your palms are facing inward as this protects the inside of the forearms from laceration and extensive damaged in the event of an unavoidable contact connection. Additionally your other hand should be in your center and up near your chin area.

CONTROL OF TARGET SIZE

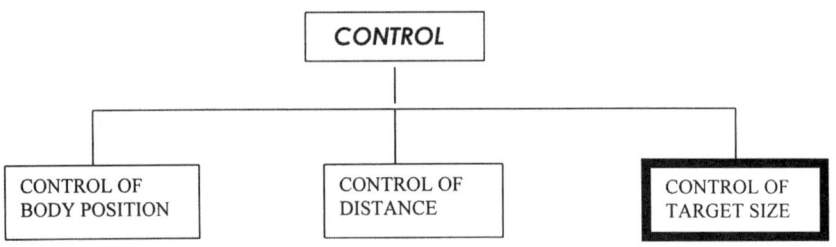

Bigger targets are easier to hit than smaller targets

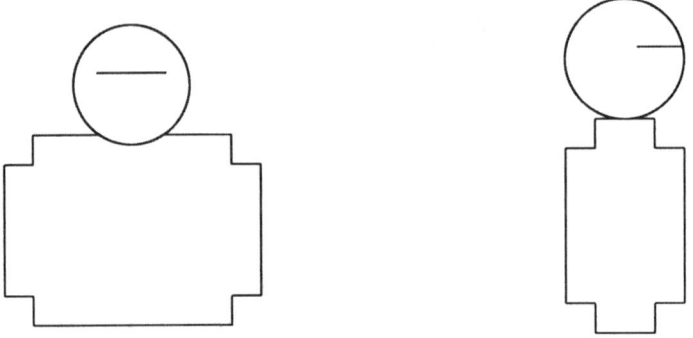

Body Pivots

Next set of motor skills is body pivots. As seen in the above diagram, the basic principle here is to reduce the size of your exposed body so that you do not expose too much of yourself as potential target area for your

Part One—The Fundamentals of Edged Weapons Defense Technology

attacker. The difference between wide and narrow target cannot be overstated. Wider is not better. Bigger targets are simply easier to hit. If you make yourself a bigger target you're increasing your chances of getting hit. If you make yourself a smaller target, then you are reducing those chances.

This segment is divided into four drills each working on the same basic skill, which is pivoting. The pivot will help to foster the energy used to deflect the on coming attack while at the same time reduce our target area as it appears to the attacker and will be employed later on to gain superior tactical position. This step will also set the groundwork for movement and mobility or footwork.

The four postures we will use for the drills are:
- Hands behind the back—pivot only.
- Hands below your belt—forearms to assist in the pivot.
- Hands above your belt—elbows to assist in the defense while pivoting.
- Hands above your belt and away from your body—Closing the Car Door position.

Body Pivot Drill #1—Body Pivot

Start with your hands behind your back. Ask your training partner to execute a slow and controlled thrust towards your stomach. Using just the body pivot try to avoid contact with the incoming training blade.

Training Partner B, with training knife, prepares for a slow and controlled thrust at Training Partner A's stomach.

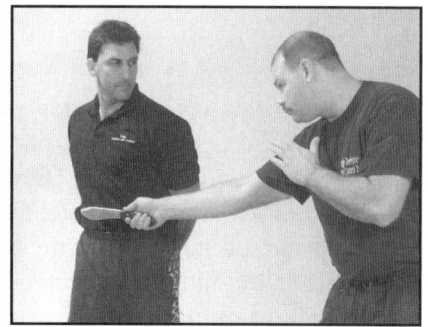

Training Partner B, with training knife, executes a slow and controlled thrust at Training Partner A's stomach. Training Partner A executes the pivot to prevent a CONTACT CONNECTION with the tip of the training knife and the target area.

Both training partners reset to their original positions.

Training Partner B, with training knife, executes a slow and controlled thrust at Training Partner A's stomach. Training Partner A executes the body pivot now in the opposite direction to prevent a CONTACT CONNECTION with the tip of the training knife and the target area. This drill is then repeated numerous times.

Body Pivot Drill #2—Forearm Pivot

Start with your hands below your waist and to your sides (a natural standing position). Ask your training partner to execute a slow and controlled thrust towards your stomach. Using the pivot try to avoid a CONTACT CONNECTION by using the forearms like flippers to deflect the incoming training blade. Be sure to keep the back of the forearms towards the knife, palms facing in, and not to extend too far beyond the outside of your body. Once the line of attack is no longer directed at your body, the deflection or parry is complete.

Part One—The Fundamentals of Edged Weapons Defense Technology

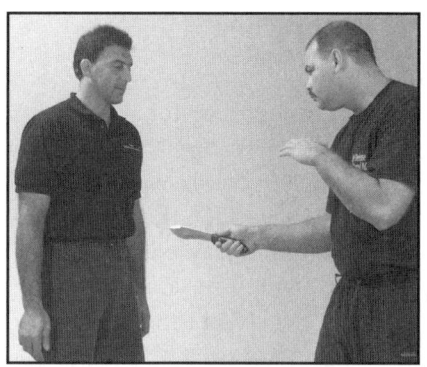

Training Partner B, with training knife, prepares for a slow and controlled thrust at Training Partner A's stomach.

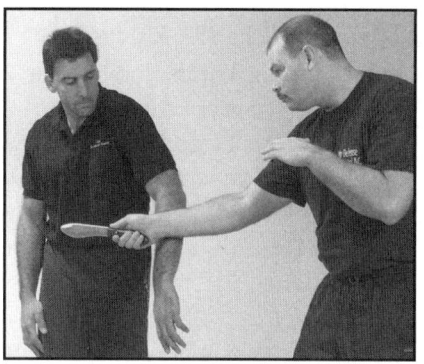

Training Partner B, with training knife, executes a slow and controlled thrust at Training Partner A's stomach. Training Partner A executes the Forearm Pivot to prevent CONTACT CONNECTION.

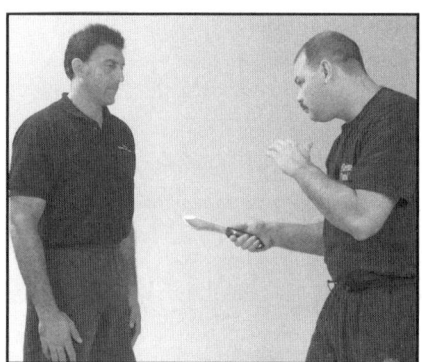

Both training partners reset to their original positions.

Training Partner B, with training knife, executes a slow and controlled thrust at Training Partner A's stomach. Training Partner A executes the forearm pivot now in the opposite direction to prevent a CONTACT CONNECTION with the tip of the training knife and the target area. This drill is then repeated numerous times.

Body Pivot Drill #3—Elbow Pivot

Start with your hands above your waist with elbows bent (as if you were picking up the phone or writing on a small notebook or for those who know what an FI position is). Slowly, your partner will execute a controlled thrust towards your stomach. Using the pivot try to avoid a CONTACT CONNECTION by using the forearms to deflect the incoming training blade. Be sure to push forcefully down and way with the bent forearm. Once the line of attack is no longer directed at your body, the deflection or parry is complete. Try not and over extend as this is a very common mistake when first learning this technique.

Training Partner B, with training knife, prepares for a slow and controlled thrust at Training Partner A's stomach.

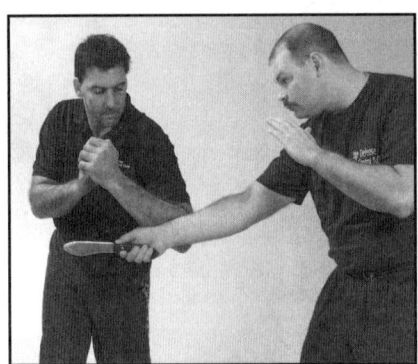

Training Partner B, with training knife, executes a slow and controlled thrust at Training Partner A's stomach. Training Partner A executes the Elbow Pivot to prevent CONTACT CONNECTION.

Part One—The Fundamentals of Edged Weapons Defense Technology

Both training partners reset to their original positions.

Training Partner B, with training knife, executes a slow and controlled thrust at Training Partner A's stomach. Training Partner A executes the elbow pivot now in the opposite direction to prevent a CONTACT CONNECTION with the tip of the training knife and the target area. This drill is then repeated numerous times.

Body Pivot Drill #4—Closing the Car Door

Start with your hands above your waist but away from your body (as if reaching out to open a window or grasp something in front of you). Slowly, your partner will execute a controlled thrust towards your stomach. Using the pivot try to avoid a CONTACT CONNECTION by using the palm to deflect the incoming training blade. Be sure to slap the attack DOWN AND AWAY from CENTER MASS and turn your CENTERLINE away from the line of attack. This is called blading the body. It narrows the target area from attack. The palm contact should be near the elbow with good solid contact and is pushed down and away in a very quick motion. The motion itself is very similar to closing a car door as you turn to walk away. Once the line of attack is no longer directed at your body, the deflection or parry is complete.

THE NAKED EDGE: THE COMPLETE GUIDE TO EDGED WEAPONS DEFENSE

Training Partner B, with training knife, prepares for a slow and controlled thrust at Training Partner A's stomach.

Training Partner B, with training knife, executes a slow and controlled thrust at Training Partner A's stomach. Training Partner A executes Closing the Car Door pushing DOWN AND AWAY to prevent CONTACT CONNECTION.

Both training partners reset to their original positions.

Training Partner B, with training knife, executes a slow and controlled thrust at Training Partner A's stomach. Training Partner A executes Closing the Car Door pivot now in the opposite direction to prevent a CONTACT CONNECTION with the tip of the training knife and the target area. This drill is then repeated numerous times.

The most important point to remember when executing "Closing the Car Door" is that your pushing hand is violently slamming the attacker's forearm down and away from your centerline. In other words you want to keep that edge and that tip as far down and away from your body as you can.

Part Two

Defending Against Non-Contact and Contact Range Attacks

Break and Clear (Non-Contact Range)

When defending against an edged weapon or any contact weapon for that matter, it is the CONTACT CONNECTION, which must be avoided at all costs. The previous section dealt with the various pivot drills employed to blade the body thus reducing the size of your opponent's target, which, if you haven't yet already realized, is your body.

This segment deals with the assessment and reaction of an attack at non-contact range and the movement required to distance yourself from the attack. Keep in mind that the potential danger of contact is just as great as the danger since the amount of time it takes to complete this attack is so very small.

This drill segment directly addresses the CONTACT CONNECTION and how to CLEAR to "SAFETY RANGE"—if you'll recall from earlier—that subjective distance determined by the defender to be a safe and negotiable distance from the attacker. The use of the 45-degree step back and away from the attacker is the key to success in this maneuver.

Break and Clear Drill #1

Gauge with your partner for non-contact range. Your training partner will then thrust slowly and in a controlled manner at or about your belt line while you respond by breaking and clearing to a SAFETY RANGE.

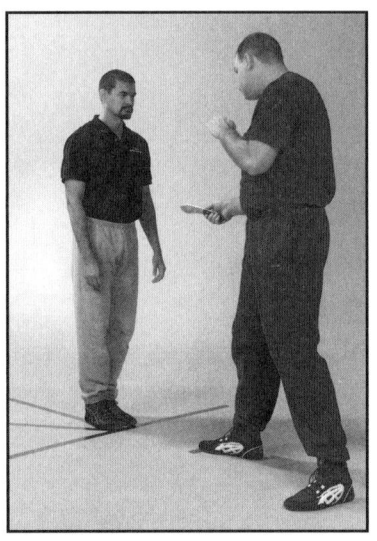

Training Partner A, after gauging distance, prepares for a slow and controlled thrust at Training Partner B's stomach.

Part Two—Defending Against Non-Contact and Contact Range Attacks

Training Partner A, with training knife, executes a slow and controlled thrust at Training Partner B's stomach. Training Partner B steps back and away at a 45-degree angle from the attack.

Break and Clear Drill #2

Gauge with your partner for non-contact range. Your training partner will then slash either forehand or backhand in a slow and controlled manner while you respond by breaking and clearing to SAFETY RANGE.

Training Partner A, after gauging distance, prepares for a slow and controlled slash at Training Partner B's neck.

The Naked Edge: The Complete Guide to Edged Weapons Defense

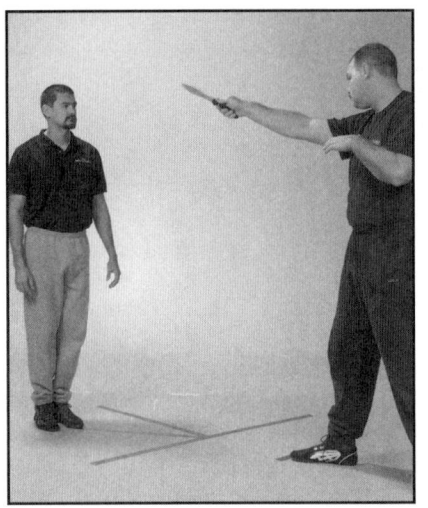 

Training Partner A, with training knife, executes a slow and controlled slash at Training Partner B's neck. Training Partner B steps back and away at a 45-degree angle from the attack and continues moving on to SAFETY RANGE.

Break and Clear Drill #3

Gauge with your partner for non-contact range. Your training partner then slashes or thrusts in a slow and controlled manner and continues moving toward you one or two steps continually swinging his training blade at random order to double-check your SAFETY RANGE.

Training Partner A, after gauging distance, prepares for a slow and controlled thrust, slash or hack at Training Partner B.

Part Two—Defending Against Non-Contact and Contact Range Attacks

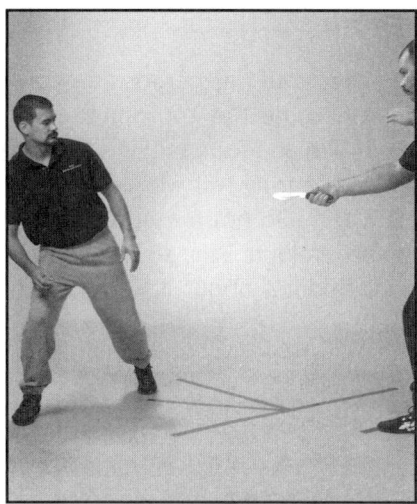 

Training Partner A, with training knife, executes a slow and controlled thrust, slash or hack at Training Partner B. Training Partner B steps back and away at a 45-degree angle from the attack and clears to safety range.

Training Partner A, with training knife, again steps forward and executes a slow and controlled thrust, slash or hack at Training Partner to check to see if he truly is at SAFETY RANGE.

Remember when executing these drills that these are intended for NON-CONTACT RANGE so don't forget to gauge for non-contact range at the beginning of each drill. Aggressively prevent the occurance of a CONTACT CONNECTION by using footwork at a 45-degree angle. Do not run backwards because, as discussed earlier, it is just a matter of time before your attacker will overrun your position (a guy running forward always will run faster than a guy running backwards). Additionally, avoid moving in a lateral direction since it takes longer for you to adjust body position than it will for your attacker to adjust his attack to your movement.

Move to the Outside

In this drill segment you will again gauge with your partner for non-contact range. Your training partner will then execute the appropriate drill attack in a slow and controlled manner and then continue moving toward you to double check your SAFETY RANGE and to truly test whether or not you ended up in a superior position (OUTSIDE). Do not forget to look at and assess your immediate surroundings and evaluate your situation—the fight's not over until your are telling your buddies about it and they're buying the beer.

The goal of Moving to the OUTSIDE is twofold. First is to avoid reengagement of a CONTACT CONNECTION and second to control distance. He who controls distance controls the fight. If you make the move and he's reacting to your actions then it is **you** who maintains control. If it's the other way around then your attacker maintains control.

By moving to the outside, as we mentioned earlier, you are moving toward superior position. When you move toward superior position you are taking action and causing a reaction by your opponent.

Being involved in an edged weapon altercation is bad enough as it is but remembering the Edged Weapon Survival Formula can give you a distinct advantage over someone who lacks formal training.

Move to the Outside Drill #1

Gauge with your partner for non-contact range. Yout training partner then thrusts in a slow and controlled manner at or about your belt line, BREAK AND CLEAR to SAFETY RANGE, move to superior position, look and asses. Basically you are applying the Edged Weapon Survival Formula.

Training Partner A, after gauging distance, prepares for a slow and controlled thrust, slash or hack at Training Partner B

Part Two—Defending Against Non-Contact and Contact Range Attacks

Training Partner A, with training knife, executes a slow and controlled thrust, slash or hack at Training Partner B. Training Partner B, steps back and away at a 45-degree angle from the attack, moves to a SUPERIOR POSITION, then LOOKS AND ASSESSES the situation.

The four steps listed below are the keys to surviving an attack at non-contact range. Each time you drill you should make sure that these elements are present and applied with great attention to detail. Additionally, only after sufficient repetitions will the actions be ingrained as second nature.

EDGED WEAPONS STREET SURVIVAL FORMULA

1. BREAK CONTACT CONNECTION
2. CLEAR TO SAFETY RANGE
3. ESTABLISH SUPERIOR POSITION
4. LOOK AND ASSESS

Defending Against Contact Range Attacks
(Break and Clear at Contact Range)

When defending against an edged weapon or any contact weapon for that matter, it is the CONTACT CONNECTION, which must be avoided at all costs.

In situations where an attacker may be at contact range, there is not enough time to react with just your feet in order to break the contact connection and clear to safety range. Many security and law enforcement personnel comment; "Well, if he's got a knife, then I'll just shoot him." The problem is that at contact range the knife is already on its way to your throat before you can even start to reach for your firearm or baton or OC spray or even to use your feet to get off the line of attack.

Examples of surprise attack at close quarters where there is not enough time for you to react with another defensive weapon or even to use your feet to step off the line of attack. At contact range, with the element of surprise on his side, the attacker always has the advantage.

The previous section dealt with breaking and clearing at non-contact range. This drill segment deals with the BREAK AND CLEAR at CONTACT RANGE. That is the application of the four pivot drills from the four arm positions added with the breaking and clearing skills. This is first done by the numbers, then by random attack. The final step is the addition of the SAFETY RANGE and the LOOK AND ASSESSES. Remember, the closer you get in a knife fight or a gunfight, or any fight for that matter, the more of you is exposed as potential target area. The goal at CONTACT RANGE is to minimize your target area and thus personal exposure.

Part Two—Defending Against Non-Contact and Contact Range Attacks

DOWN AND AWAY DRILLS

1. Body Pivot

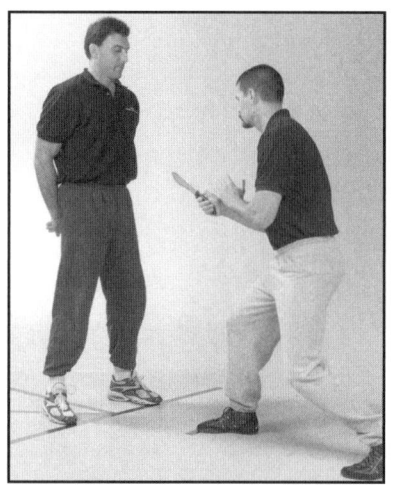

Training Partner A, with training knife, prepares for a slow and controlled thrust at Training Partner B's stomach.

Training Partner A, with training knife, executes a slow and controlled thrust at Training Partner B's stomach. Training Partner B executes the pivot to prevent CONTACT CONNECTION.

Training Partner B then steps back and away at a 45-degree angle from the attack, moves to a SUPERIOR POSITION, then LOOKS AND ASSESSES the situation.

2. Forearm Pivot

Training Partner A, with training knife, prepares for a slow and controlled thrust at Training Partner B's stomach.

Training Partner A, with training knife, executes a slow and controlled thrust at Training Partner B's stomach. Training Partner B executes the Forearm pivot to prevent CONTACT CONNECTION.

Training Partner B then steps back and away at a 45-degree angle from the attack, moves to a SUPERIOR POSITION, then LOOKS AND ASSESSES the situation.

Part Two—Defending Against Non-Contact and Contact Range Attacks

3. Elbow Pivot

Training Partner A, with training knife, prepares for a slow and controlled thrust at Training Partner B's stomach.

Training Partner A, with training knife, executes a slow and controlled thrust at Training Partner B's stomach. Training Partner B executes the Elbow pivot to prevent CONTACT CONNECTION.

Training Partner B then steps back and away at a 45-degree angle from the attack, moves to a SUPERIOR POSITION, then LOOKS AND ASSESSES the situation.

4. Closing the Car Door

Training Partner A, with training knife, prepares for a slow and controlled thrust at Training Partner B's stomach.

Training Partner A, with training knife, executes a slow and controlled thrust at Training Partner B's stomach. Training Partner B executes "Closing the Car Door" to prevent CONTACT CONNECTION.

Training Partner B then steps back and away at a 45-degree angle from the attack, moves to a SUPERIOR POSITION, then LOOKS AND ASSESSES the situation.

Part Two—Defending Against Non-Contact and Contact Range Attacks

Down and away Drill Summary—An Addendum

DOWN AND AWAY SERIES 1—The Four Pivot drills (body, forearm, elbow, close the car door) with the 45-Degree step by the numbers: Drill 1, Drill 2, Drill 3, and Drill 4, and repeat.

DOWN AND AWAY SERIES 2—The Four Pivot drills (body, forearm, elbow, close the car door) with the 45-Degree step in Random sequence. (Drill 2, Drill 4, Drill 1, Drill 3, Drill 1, Drill 1, Drill 3, Drill 2, Drill 4, etc.)

DOWN AND AWAY SERIES 3—The Four Pivot drills (body, forearm, elbow, close the car door) with the 45-Degree step, then add BREAK AND CLEAR, assume SAFETY RANGE/SUPERIOR POSITION, and LOOK AND ASSESS by the numbers.

DOWN AND AWAY SERIES 4—The Four Pivots (body, forearm, elbow, close the car door) with the 45-Degree step, then add BREAK AND CLEAR, assume SAFETY RANGE/SUPERIOR POSITION, and LOOK AND ASSESS in Random sequence.

At this particular point in your training you should be able to accept low-line attacks from your training partner at controlled speeds at random and properly execute the Edged Weapons Survival Formula. Only after you feel extremely comfortable with execution of this formula (especially when applied to DOWN AND AWAY SERIES 4) should you attempt to move to the next section.

High Line Attacks

Now that we have covered the low line attacks you are fully prepared to venture forth into the world of low line attack training. It is, however, recommended that you inform any would-be attackers in the street that you are only willing to accept attacks on the low line and that any attacks above the waist will not be tolerated.

In reality it is just as likely that you will be slashed across the throat, as it is that you will be stabbed in the belly. In fact they will likely try both! So how would you handle attacks to the high line?

High line attacks are basically addressed in much the same way as attacks to the low line. For low line attacks, the key is DOWN AND AWAY as the attack was already on the low line and half way where it needs to be away from your center mass, now because of it's movement toward your vitals from the high line of attack you must endeavor to keep the weapon QuickShield™ from its target. That target of course is you and just like in the DOWN AND AWAY drills you are still dealing with an attack at CONTACT RANGE.

In the CONTACT RANGE low line attacks we used the four different pivots. On the high line defense we will use THE TURN and QuickShield™, which we presented, in the earlier. Key points for proper use of these two basic gross motor skills are that you will need to add a slight "pop' using your secondary hand to the attacker's weapon arm to facilitate a good break and then immediately break the CONTACT CONNECTION and follow up with movement to SAFETY RANGE and finally LOOK AND ASSESS.

QuickShield™ Drill #1

Gauge with your partner for CONTACT RANGE. Your partner then slashes a forehand toward your head. You are caught on the inside. Execute TURN ONE WAY and QuickShield™ and pop attacking forearm with your support hand. Then your partner slashes at you with a backhand in which case you are caught on the outside. Execute TURN ONE WAY (the other way) and QuickShield™ and pop with the support hand. This drill is executed without foot movement to develop timing. A quick glance back to review the sections on TURN ONE WAY and QuickShield™ gross motor skills is a good idea to keep the key skill points fresh in your mind when training in this section. Be certain each step (such as chin tucked, second hand raised, etc.,) is properly maintained when you execute those elements in this drill.

Training partner delivers a slow and controlled forehand slash to your head. Execute TURN ONE WAY and QuickShield™ plus aggressively slapping the inside of the attacking weapon arm to stop his momentum.

Training partner delivers a slow and controlled backhand slash to your head. Execute TURN ONE WAY (now it's the other way) and QuickShield™ plus aggressively slapping the outside of the attacking weapon arm to stop his momentum.

Part Two—Defending Against Non-Contact and Contact Range Attacks

Repeat these steps over and over again WITHOUT footwork to develop response for situations where you cannot or are unable to use footwork to escape from a contact range attack on the high line. This will also develop both timing and placement. As you become more comfortable with this drill, ask your training partner to increase both speed and power.

QuickShield™ Drill #2

Gauge with your partner for CONTACT RANGE. Your partner then slashes a forehand toward your head. You are caught on the inside. Execute TURN ONE WAY and QuickShield™ and pop incoming weapon arm with your support hand. Now BREAK AND CLEAR, move to the outside, and LOOK AND ASSESS. Your partner will continue to chase you down to ensure that you have in fact established SUPERIOR POSITION. Repeat the drill on the backhand slash line.

Training partner delivers a slow and controlled forehand slash to your head. Execute TURN ONE WAY and QuickShield™ plus aggressively slapping the inside of the attacking weapon arm to stop his momentum.

Immediately upon slowing his momentum (breaking the contact connection), push off and step back and away at a 45-degree angle from the attack (clear to safety range), move to a SUPERIOR POSITION, then LOOK AND ASSESSES.

Training partner delivers a slow and controlled backhand slash to your head. Execute TURN ONE WAY (now the other way) and QuickShield™ plus aggressively slapping the outside of the attacking weapon arm to stop his momentum.

Immediately upon slowing his momentum (breaking the contact connection), step back and push away at a 45-degree angle from the attack (clear to safety range), move to a SUPERIOR POSITION, then LOOK AND ASSESSES.

Elbow Control

Up to now, we've studied how to handle an edged weapon attack at NON-CONTACT and CONTACT Ranges using the BREAK AND CLEAR and MOVE TO THE OUTSIDE as an immediate reactive response. This is optimum in any edged weapon encounter. However, in the real world, the option to break the CONTACT CONNECTION and make distance from your threat (clear to SAFETY RANGE) is not always available. In certain situations it is necessary to close in and handle the situation at Extreme Close Quarters (ECQ). In these precarious situations the decision must be made of when to go in and when to get out Intellectually it's a rather deductive decision, if you don't have a choice or cannot get away, then your only option is to go in. Practically speaking, when you are under tremendous stress and adrenaline is pumping through your nervous system, it may not be such an easy task to make that decision in a split second.

If you must close in, then you must immediately establish control. To explain the concept of elbow control let's first start again with the low line thrust. In this example of "going in" we of course strive to position ourselves on the outside for obvious reasons as we discussed in earlier chapters. Executing any of the body pivot techniques will easily establish your movement and position to the outside. Once you're there and cannot

Part Two— Defending Against Non-Contact and Contact Range Attacks

BREAK AND CLEAR to SAFETY RANGE, the next best thing you can do is to establish control of CENTERLINE and momentum of the incoming attack.

> "He who control the center controls the fight..."
> —Bruce Lee

To demonstrate how power is applied against an attack and the amount of control present we will go through three experiments.

Experiment #1

Ask your training partner to just stand there with his hands by his side. Standing on his OUTSIDE grab his wrist and push forward to try and make him take a step.

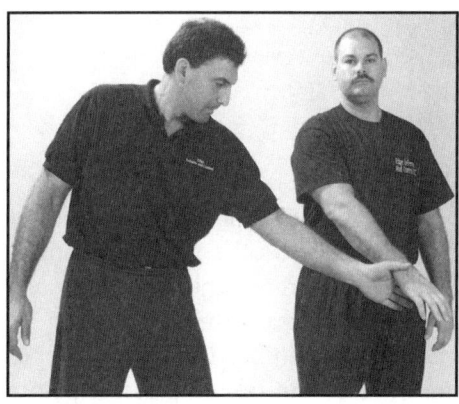

Little to no influence or control of his center mass is applied when applying power to the wrist.

Experiment #2

Now take your hand and form the letter "C" with the thumb and fingers. Firmly grasp his elbow (just above the elbow and at the bottom of his ticeps) with your hand in the PALM UP position and push. You should notice that he becomes a little bit more off-balance than when you applied power to his wrist and may even need to take small step at this point to regain his balance.

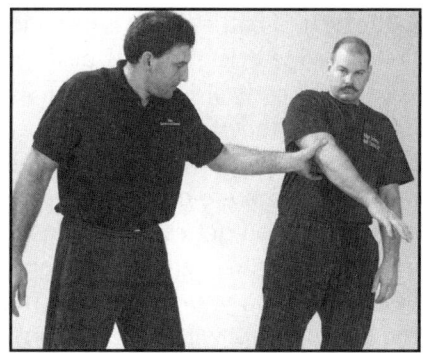

Additional influence and control is accomplished when applying power to the elbow.

Experiment #3
Lastly, take it one step closer and apply power to his shoulder and push toward his center. You'll find that when power is applied closer to his center it has more influence over the entire body.

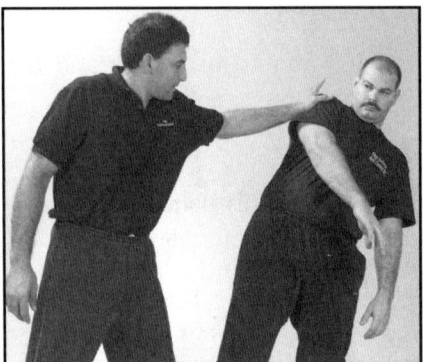

A great deal of influence is attained when applying power closer to center.

Pain Compliance versus Mechanical Compliance

Compliance has a greater effect than influence and facilitates control. Some martial arts are based upon pain compliance and others on mechanical compliance. Simply, some hurt you to make you move the way they want while others place you in such a way that your resistance is minimized by that position or the generation of motion. Remember that some people have a pain threshold that's off the map. We cannot rely on pressure points that waste valuable time in finding that "exact spot" that causes pain only in the heat of battle—pain is just another element of conflict.

In edged defense it is best for the operator to establish mechanical advantage control holds that utilize position, movement, the attacker's body, resistance, and motion to achieve control. Pain may and often does, just make a person really, really mad and is often unpredictable in individuals who are on drugs or in a state of emotional distress.

When you get caught in an ECQ situation you're usually not expecting it and you're generally caught by surprise. Due to the nature of an ECQ altercation your hands are most likely going to instinctively react by moving upward without any conscious thought. Additionally, there are four positions in which you may find yourself with eyes and mouth wide open with a quickened pulse and shallow breathing.

Part Two—Defending Against Non-Contact and Contact Range Attacks

You're just walking along minding your own business when all of a sudden some shadowy figure jumps out from the bushes with a rusted steak knife and you're there, caught at ECQ with your hands down by your side and shocked out of your wits. You could end up literally "frozen" in your tracks.

You're walking along minding your own business when all of a sudden you notice that someone is coming rapidly into ECQ range wielding an edged weapon. Instinctively one hand may rise up.

You're walking along minding your own business when all of a sudden you notice that someone is coming rapidly into ECQ range wielding an edged weapon. Instinctively the other hand may rise up.

You're walking along minding your own business when all of a sudden you notice that someone is coming rapidly into ECQ range wielding an edged weapon. Instinctively both hands may rise up.

Bottom line is, until you're in it you're never going to know how you will react. The best preparation you can make is to train for as many scenarios as possible that would more closely resemble a realistic situation in which you could find yourself at extreme close quarters—based on your natural and instinctive reactions.

Opposing Strengths

The human arm has a limited amount of strength, and what ever that strength might be it is certainly less than the entire body. This is a case of a part being less than the whole. To establish control over the opponents attacking limb we use the overall power and strength of the entire body.

Strength comes from muscle mass. Whoever has the greater amount of activated muscle mass has the greatest strength. The large muscle mass of the defenders upper body is employed against the attacker's limb. Basically, it is a battle between the large muscles of the back and the small ones of the arm. This strength combined with the fact that our body outweighs the attackers limb, allows us to establish stable control of the opponent.

Elbow Control Drill #1

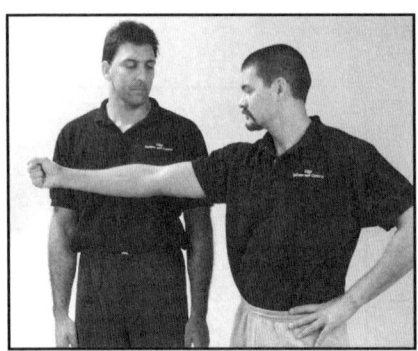

Training Partner stands comfortably and offers his arm for training. You are standing on the outside position with hands by your side. In advanced training your partner may begin this drill with a low line thrust.

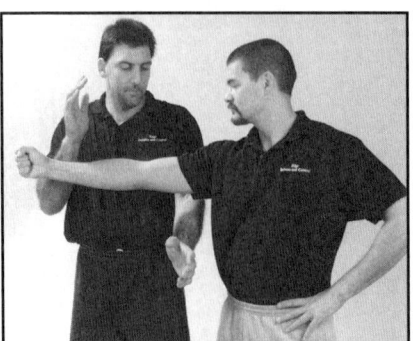

Take your near arm, raise it up under your partners extended arm and at the same time move your far arm against the outside of your partners same extended arm.

Part Two—Defending Against Non-Contact and Contact Range Attacks

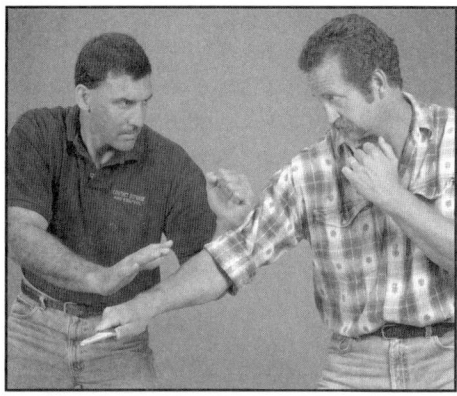

Taking care not to bring the knife edge close to your body, continue Moving the inside hand until it is resting along the outside of your partners triceps.

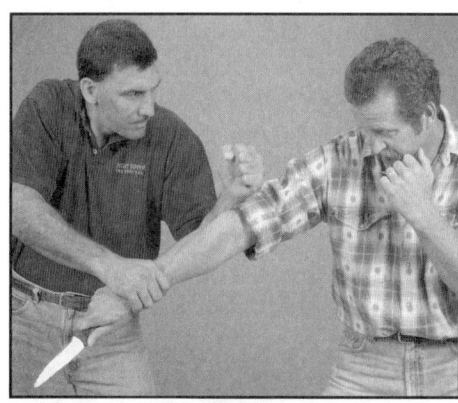

Acquire a full grip (thumb wrapped all the way around) on the wrist and at the same time applying pressure ABOVE the elbow joint.

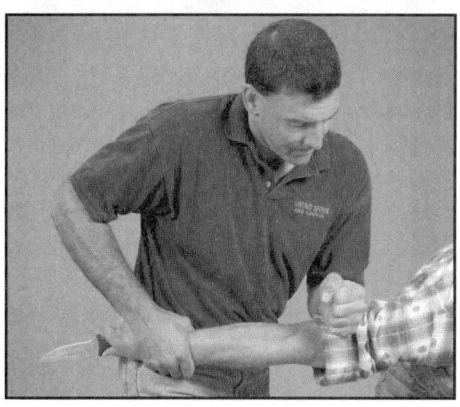

Now "Velcro" the hand to your hipbone at the belt level and continue to add pressure using your forearm against the area just above his elbow joint.

This technique ensures you a position of advantage located on the OUTSIDE. At any time if things got ugly you could simply push off, disengage and step away off at 45 degrees.

Next, simply apply your body weight as if sitting in a chair by stepping forward with your inside leg.

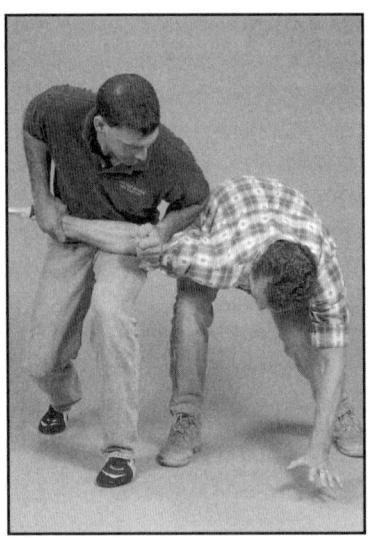

Bend your inside leg so as to end up placing your inside knee firmly against the deck and simultaneously place your outside foot flat to form a stable three-point base.

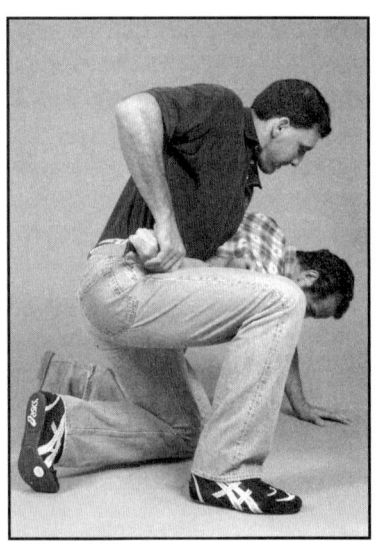

It is imperative to form a solid three-point base using both feet and one knee to form a solid triangular base where you are placed in a position of mechanical advantage.

Part Two—Defending Against Non-Contact and Contact Range Attacks

By maintaining the "Velcro" of his wrist to your beltline at the hip as well as your body weight against the control point above his elbow joint, you have effectively controlled the weapon arm while maintaining a position of advantage to the outside.

Repeat these above steps a number of times until you feel comfortable with STRAIGH ARM BAR position on the OUTSIDE. These drills were designed to develop position and placement of both the near and far arm for control of the elbow at extreme close quarters for the purpose of controlling the CONTACT CONNECTION and immobilizing the attack using opposing strengths—that is, your overall body weight and strength versus your opponents arm strength.

Elbow Control Drill #2

Your training partner again offers his arm and holding a training blade for purposes of the drill. Execute Elbow Control # 1. Now that you are comfortable with this position, the next step is to control your opponent should he begin to resist your control.

Once you've attained a comfortable degree of proficiency, ask your partner to mildly resist once you've got the hold on and try to pull either up or out while keeping his arm straight (later we will address the issue of handling the situation if he decides to bend his arm at the elbow).

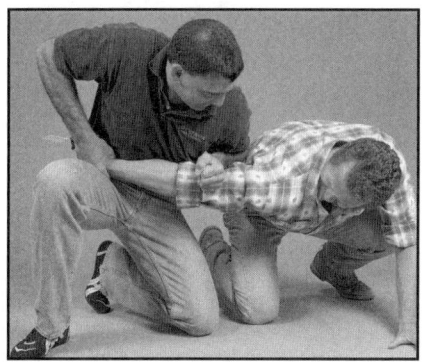

He begins to resist as you have begun to control him from the outside position.

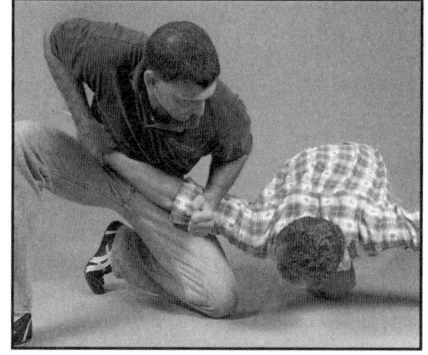

Take one big step with your outside leg and slide your inside knee behind for support.

Gradually, as you increase skill, it will be difficult if at all possible for him to remove his arm from under the pressure of your body weight and position. Remember not to start out thrashing violently about. The purpose of these drills is to establish foundation by repetition.

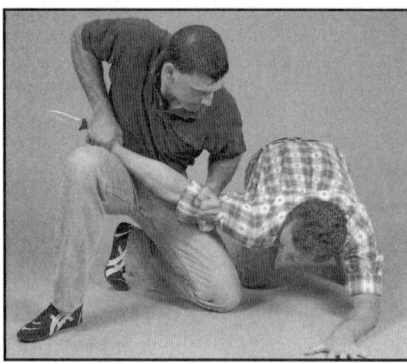

If he continues to resist or tries to re-post with his free arm, then simply take another deep step off on a forty-five degree angle forward and slide your other leg behind.

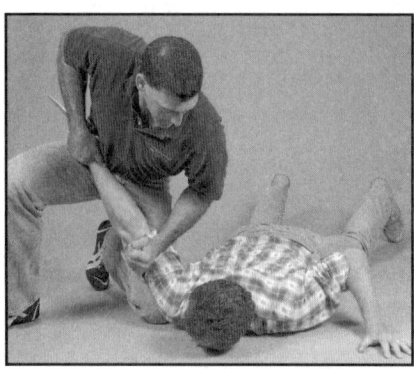

This will break his balance and at the same time ensure you a stable platform from which to further control and immobilize the weapon arm if necessary.

At the completion of this movement, unable to post, he will end up in what is known in the training industry as a "face down stabilization."

It is very important to be careful when training these drills with your partner as they are designed, of course, to work when applied correctly, so take good care of your partner's elbow and shoulder joints as good training partners are difficult to find!

At this point in the game it is usually the case that you have successfully controlled the contact connection and effectively immobilized your opponent. However, in some cases he may continue to struggle

Part Two—Defending Against Non-Contact and Contact Range Attacks

and attempt to break free. In the event of a continued struggle in the "face down stabilization" position, there are a few options you can add to your toolbox.

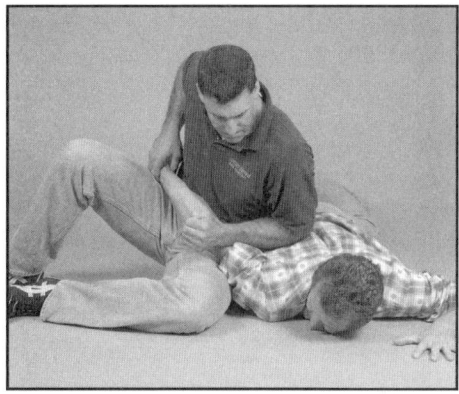

In the event that he offers additional resistance from the "face down stabilization" position, you can simply pop your inside leg out and sit up close against his armpit.

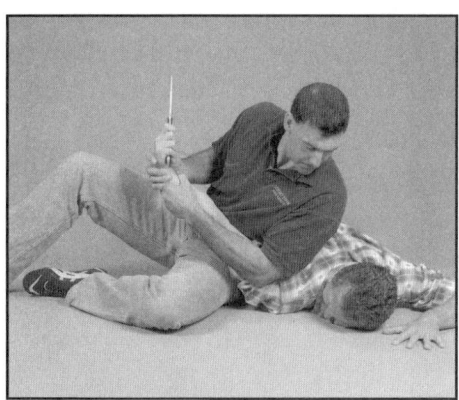

By using your legs to push your hips up under his armpit (while keeping the weapon safely away) this applies tremendous pressure to his shoulder.

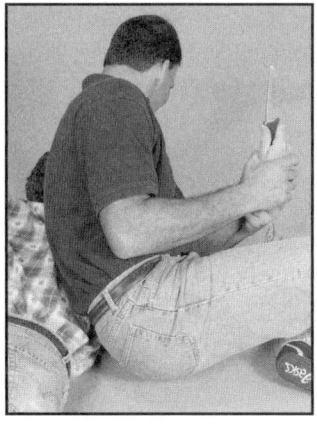

With his rotator cuff pinned to the deck using the weight of your body and pushing in with your legs there is a measurable degree of discomfort which adds to the effectiveness of mechanical compliance.

There are a few key points which should be illustrated to clarify optimum position of control.

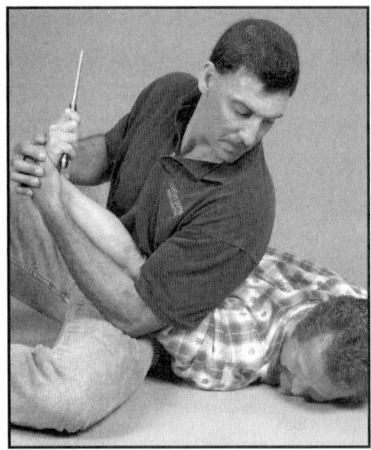

Be sure that your hips are up close and tight against the ribs and up on a 45-degree diagonal into his armpit as this is what directs the pressure of your body against his rotator cuff to the deck.

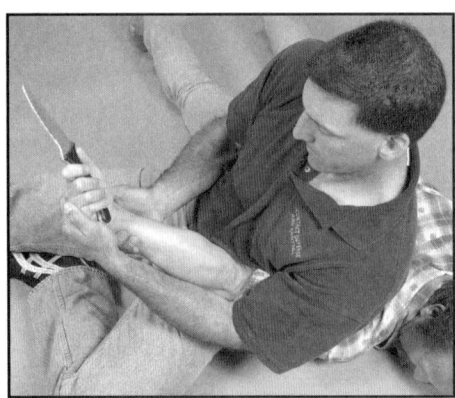

Next, position your hands in such a manner as to apply UPWARD pressure. This movement applies additional pressure to the elbow as well as reinforces pressure against the shoulder.

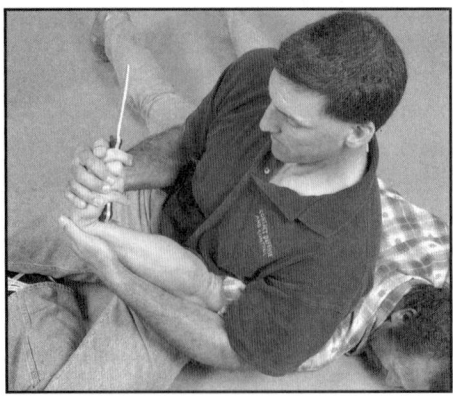

Finally if you are concerned about the weapon which may still be in his hand, you have the option of moving your hands up to bend his wrist thus applying additional pressure to both the elbow and the shoulder.

Part Two—Defending Against Non-Contact and Contact Range Attacks

Repeat these above steps a number of times until you feel comfortable. Remember again that these are drills. Later on we will apply these in dynamic training scenarios to develop more advanced skills. But for now, please try to keep this a slow and controlled training module until these drills can be executed efficiently, with control and with little or no effort.

Elbow Control Problem Solving

There may be times when the elbow control seems weak or that he may be able to escape. There are a few fine tune points that may remedy the problem.

1. Have you properly applied the "Velcro" technique by securing his wrist to your hip bone at the belt line? If any space or loose areas between your body and your training partner's extended arm, then remove any space or slack and fasten your secured grip as if your life depended upon it—especially if this were a real world situation.

 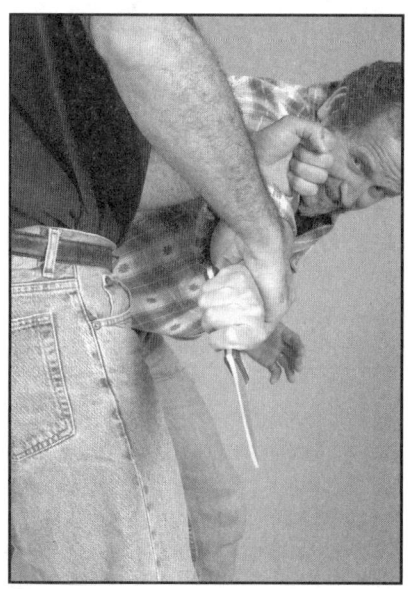

Correct position of your partner's wrist in the "Velcro" position.   *Incorrect position of your partner's wrist in "Velcro" position.*

2. When applying the takedown is his shoulder above your beltline or below it? It is imperative that his shoulder be at a point below your beltline as this assures the fulcrum point necessary to facilitate the displacement of your body weight in movement. Without the alignment of his shoulder at or BELOW your beltline you may experience difficulties with further manipulation and control of your opponent.

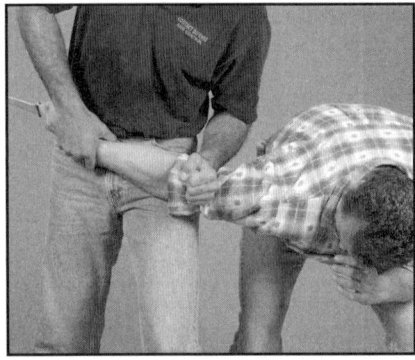

Correct position of opponent's shoulder at or below your beltline for optimum leverage and control.

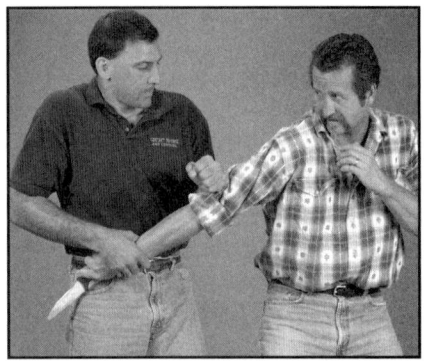

Incorrect position of your opponent's shoulder—too high for practical application.

3. Is the opposing strength too relaxed or not up tight against your partner's armpit? Remember, similar to the grappling game "Space equal escape, contact equals control." The same applies here in these control and immobilization scenarios.

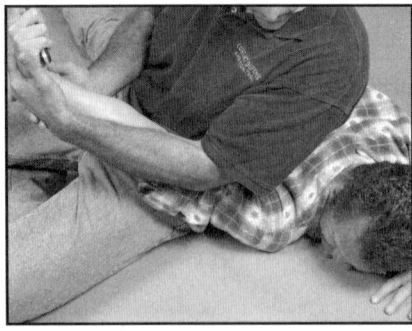

Correct position of your hip against your partners armpit.

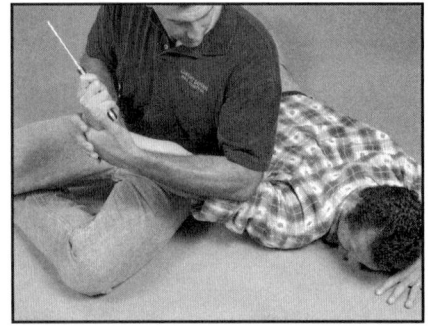

Incorrect position of your hip against your partner's armpit.

PART TWO—DEFENDING AGAINST NON-CONTACT AND CONTACT RANGE ATTACKS

Elbow Control Drill #3

In Elbow Control Drill #1 you have demonstrated taking control of your opponent's weapon arm from a position of advantage and using your body weight as an OPPOSING STRENGTH to gain mechanical advantage in this self-defense situation.

In Elbow Control Drill #2—an extension of Elbow Control Drill #1—you have demonstrated taking additional control as well as balance away from your opponent in the event of a possible struggle and thus resulting in a FACE DOWN STABILIZATION position.

This next drill is a solution provided in the event that your opponent forcibly resists your attempts at both Elbow Control Drill #1 and Elbow Control Drill #2. In the event that he may bend his weapon arm and start to push you in the opposite direction in which you intend to take him, it is necessary to have a response adequate to match his efforts.

Perhaps you were somewhat successful in application of Elbow Control Drill #1.

However, attempting to go any further proves to be a problem as he bends his elbow and attempts escape in the opposite direction.

Step one—don't panic. If he wants to toward the opposite direction, then that's the way he needs to go. Subsequent movements provide an optimum solution to accommodating your opponent toward his new direction.

He begins to apply additional upward pressure as he bends his arm in attempt to break free and continue his attack.

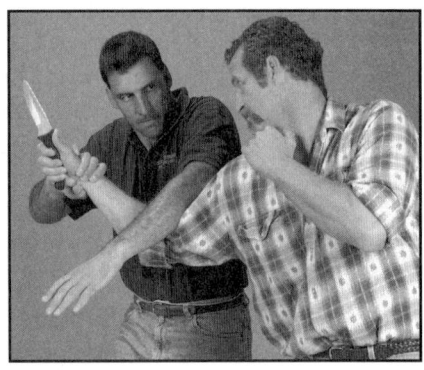

Simply maintain your fast grip around his wrist and begin to weave your other arm over his extended weapon arm.

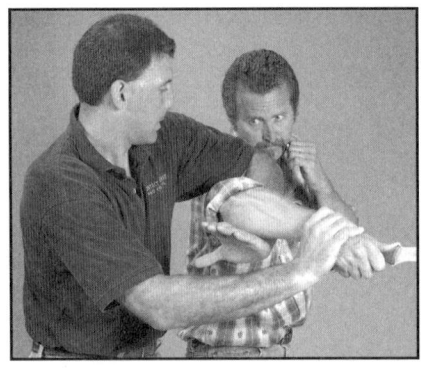

Continue to weave your free arm over and then under his extended arm maintaining a fast grip.

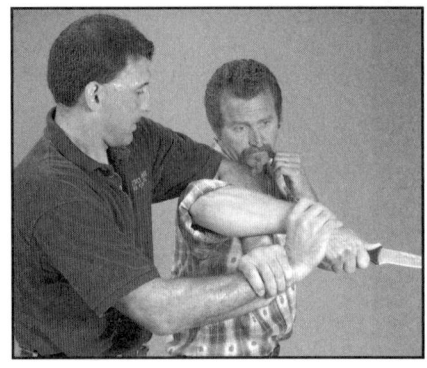

Once you've completed the weave over and under, then grasp your own wrist in a full grip fashion commonly known as a figure 4 lock.

Part Two—Defending Against Non-Contact and Contact Range Attacks

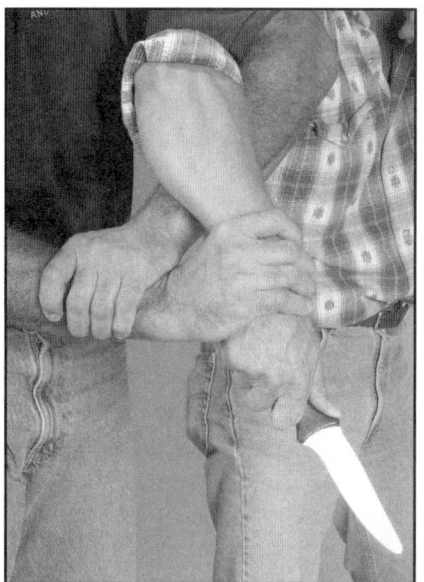

Proper configuration of the figure 4 lock.

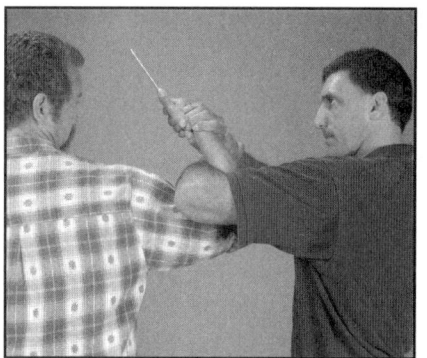

At this point begin to straighten your body upward and maintain a good stance with your feet and lower body.

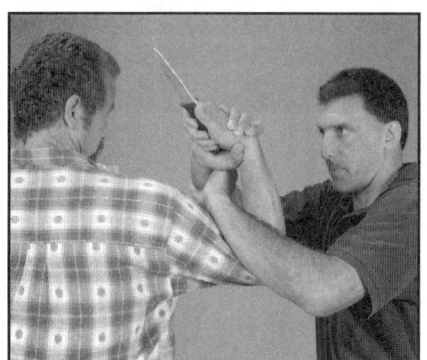

Turn toward the opposite direction and maintain momentum as you pivot.

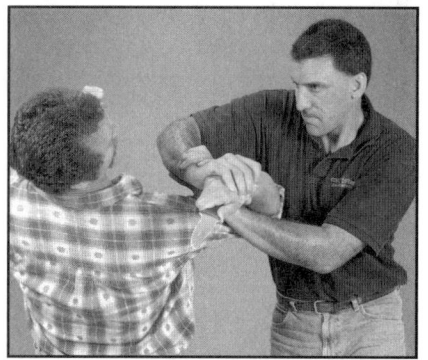

Begin to take him backward in the opposite direction.

Elbow Control Drill # 3 will cause your opponent to move backward toward the other direction and become off balance. The course material for this section ends at this step. However, as a well-rounded martial artist or defensive tactics practitioner, you've probably trained in some sort of hand-to-hand training, this should be a very familiar position from which to work. A couple of suggestions would be a takedown or a control to submission for example.

As you've probably figured out by now, there is an extreme amount of pressure applied to your training partner's joints. We all want to, of course, train with reality, however, we must at the same time be considerate of our training partners and practice safely with respects to your partner's body.

A suggested follow-up to Elbow Control Drill #3 is what is commonly known in the training industry as a "Face Up Stabilization."

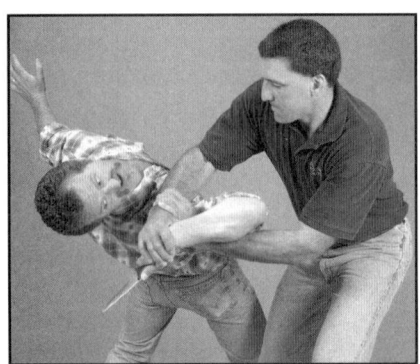

To acquire the FACE UP STABILIZATION POSITION, simply continue moving in the same direction.

Begin to drop your body weight again as if you were about to sit in a chair.

Part Two—Defending Against Non-Contact and Contact Range Attacks

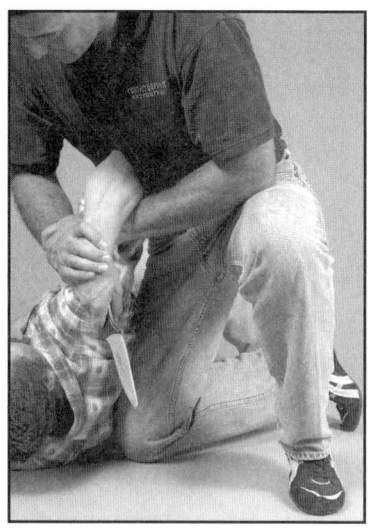

Again come to the inside knee and keep his body perpendicular to the deck as this will prevent roll-out.

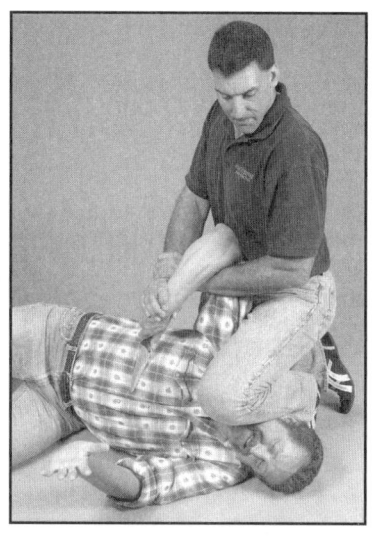

Maintain your secure grip. Turn and place your upward knee on the side of his head for additional control.

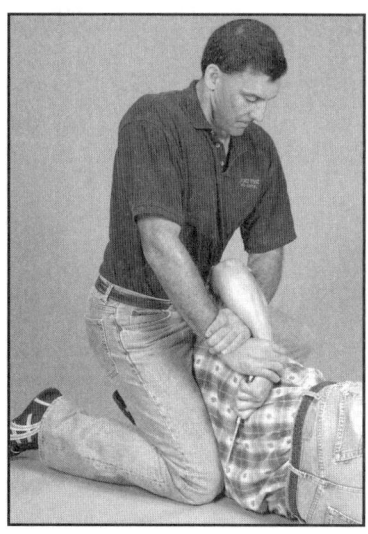

To further secure the weapon, simply swing it around to his back.

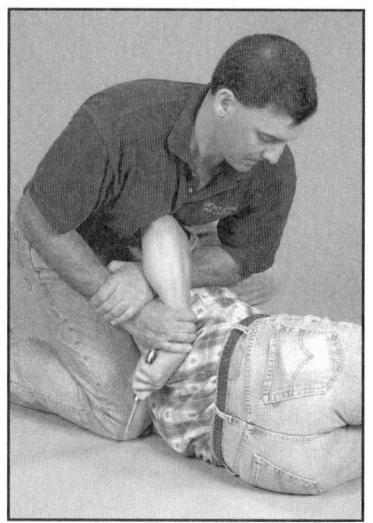

By then resting on his elbow with your upper torso, you can secure and control his weapon arm.

At this stage of the game you have successfully executed a FACE UP STABILIZATION and have controlled and immobilized your attacker employing Elbow Control Drill #3.

According to one of the greatest DT instructors and Martial Artists to ever walk the planet—Guru Dan Inosanto, techniques are much like clothing in that certain techniques will fit some practitioners comfortably, but may not fit others at all. The fourth and final elbow control drill is provided for those who do not feel comfortable with either of the first three.

Aside form specific technique, it is important to note that at no time are you REQUIRED to engage with your opponent at extreme close quarters in an edged weapon altercation! Remember, the safest place to be in ANY edged (or contact weapon for that matter) weapon scenario is far away and minimally at a position of advantage. If you're able to break and clear from the contact connection and move to superior position, then get out of there or get something between you and harms way!!

These techniques and training drills are provided in the event that there ARE NBO REMAINING OPTIONS and that you MUST engage your opponent, for whatever reason, in an edged weapon altercation at extreme close quarters and you seek to gain the mechanical advantage.

As mentioned earlier, your height, reach, weight, skill level and personal preference versus your opponent will determine which technique best fits you. In the rare event that none of the above techniques fit your personal profile, there is an additional option that was passed down to me directly from my Eskrima Master Punong Guro Edgar G. Sulite, which for purposes of continuity within this manuscript, I have given the title "Elbow Control Drill #4.

Elbow Control Drill #4

In this drill, have your partner, using a training knife, gauge for CONTACT RANGE. Your partner will then thrust forward toward your belt line in a safe and controlled manner. Use any one of the pivot drills (body pivot, forearm, elbow or close the car door) to gain outside position (position of advantage) and transition to an UNDER/ OVER control hold.

Part Two—Defending Against Non-Contact and Contact Range Attacks

In this example, your hands happen to begin QuickShield™ from your body, so you'll want to execute a "Close the Car Door" to get to the outside.

As the incoming thrust is in motion, execute a clean "Close the Car Door" while moving to the outside.

Maintaining control of the attacking weapon arm, continue to push down and away from your center and begin the UNDER/ OVER movement by placing your near arm under your opponent's triceps.

Execute UNDER/ OVER and remember to keep good form in controlling the weapon arm by using opposing strength.

The Naked Edge: The Complete Guide to Edged Weapons Defense

Pull your arms together and grab your elbows thus immobilizing his weapon arm.

Turn near shoulder forward taking control of his balance.

Step with near leg into his centerline and takedown to submission.

The Next Step

At this time you may apply each pivot drill defense randomly based on the energy, speed and position that is supplied by your training partner. The key element to this training is to be able to transition to one of the elbow controls from your outside position.

Much later in your training, once you've mastered the elbow control, you may want to ask our training partner to go at you just a bit more vigorously and try to escape to test the validity of your control hold and position.

PART TWO—DEFENDING AGAINST NON-CONTACT AND CONTACT RANGE ATTACKS

Low Line Elbow Control Drill training format:
1. Repeat Elbow Control Drills 1–4 in numerical order.
2. Random repetitions of Elbow Control Drills 1–4.
3. Training partner moves a bit more aggressively to adjust your reactive response appropriately.

Elbow Control (High Line Attacks)

Now let's address the high line CONTACT RANGE attack. When an attack is launched with violent intent and at high speed to the head your natural reaction is to raise your hands to meet the attack. Not unlike the reaction of raising your hands to catch a set of keys that someone tosses at you from across the room with little warning. That is the reason why TURN ONE WAY and QuickShield™ work so well as a defense. They differ very little from the natural response of the body. Defensive tactics that are gross body skills and based on natural motions are most likely to be applied as a response in a conflict situation.

High Line Attack Elbow Control Drill #1

Training partner gauges for CONTACT RANGE. Starting from the HIGH CLOSED position he slowly slashes a controlled backhand toward your face with the training tool in his hand. Here, you execute TURN ONE WAY and THE QuickShield™ and transition directly into UNDER/OVER as we studied above. The remainder of the technique is also the same as above where, once you have successfully secured the weapon arm, you step in with the near foot to take control of his CENTER MASS.

Training partner delivers a slow and controlled backhand slash along the highline to your head area. Both your hands instinctively rise.

The Naked Edge: The Complete Guide to Edged Weapons Defense

Execute TURN ONE WAY and QuickShield™. However in this scenario, there is no time to use your legs to break and clear and get to the outside. So instead of getting out your only option is to go in.

Maintain control of the weapon arm and initiate any of the four Elbow Control Drills. In this particular example Elbow Control Drill #4 (the UNDER/OVER) is demonstrated.

Remember when executing UNDER/OVER to keep opposing pressure on the attacking arm— one going up and one going down.

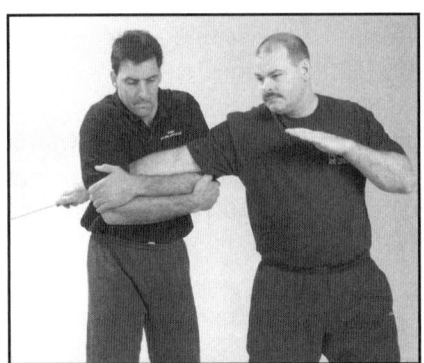

Bring arms together grasping your elbows and pulling tightly into your center so that the weapon arm is immobilized.

Part Two—Defending Against Non-Contact and Contact Range Attacks

Turn near shoulder inward to affect his balance.

Step with near leg into his cente line taking him down or to submission.

In this next scenario, the attacker comes at you with the same High Line backhand slash to your head. However, this time execute your reactive response as illustrated, followed by Elbow Control Drill #1 (Velcro Arm Bar) and then by taking control of his CENTER MASS to takedown or submission.

Training partner again initiates attack with delivery of slow and controlled high-line backhand slash to the head area.

Execute TURN ONE WAY and QuickShield™ getting to the outside position. However, in this training scenario there is no option to BREAK and CLEAR and get to SAFETY RANGE— your only option is to go in.

103

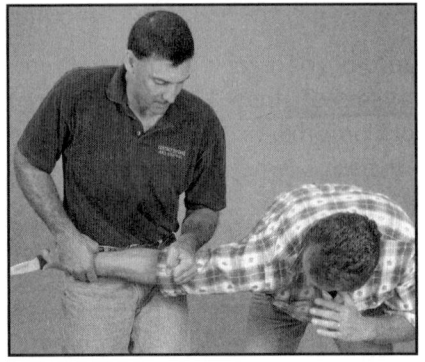

Begin execution of Elbow Control #1.

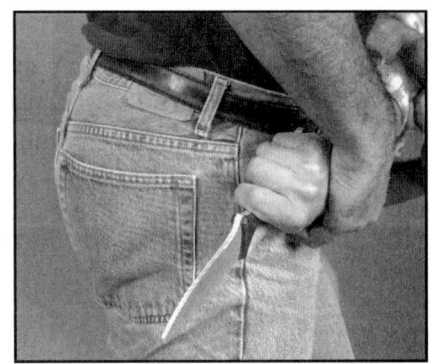

Remember to Velcro his hand tight to your beltline.

Immediately use your body weight to leverage him downward and to take his balance away.

If necessary transition into Elbow Control #2.

It may be further necessary to take him directly into a FACE DOWN STABILIZATION position from here.

Part Two—Defending Against Non-Contact and Contact Range Attacks

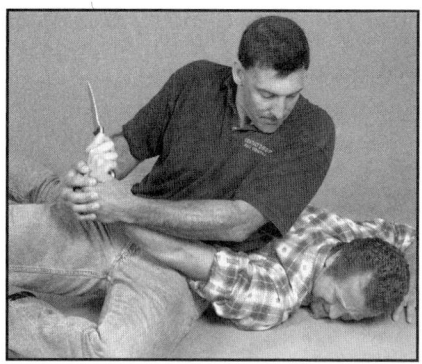

Prone him out and gain superior position by controlling his shoulder with your hips.

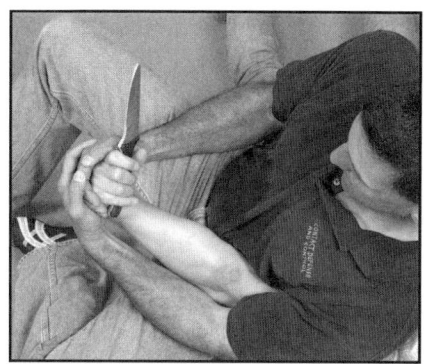

Secure the weapon arm as necessary to your situation.

At this stage you may be ready for additional dynamic scenario training. You may ask your partner to deliver either a low line thrust or a highline backhander slash. Receiving either of these deliveries you should be able to at this point, transition from basic defense (either low-line defense—DOWN AND AWAY or highline defense—QuickShield™) to any one of the four Elbow Controls as outlined above.

As an example for training, ask your partner to deliver you a low line thrust. Next, apply any of the low-line defenses (body pivot, forearm, elbow or close the car door) and then transition to any one of the Elbow Controls.

Next, ask your partner to deliver you a highline backhand slash. Apply the QuickShield™ and then transition to any one of the Elbow Controls.

As you may have already discovered, these basic defenses and Elbow Controls work fine for low-line and outside attacks. After all, the best position, as we have discussed, is to get to the outside. However, thee may be times when we are denied access to the outside—especially when mobility and space is limited and you get caught ion the INSIDE. Let's take a look at this most undesirable scenario

High Line Attack—Elbow Control Drill #2

Training partner gauges for CONTACT RANGE. Starting from the HIGH OPEN position he slowly slashes a forehand toward your face with a training blade in his hand. Here, you execute a TURN ONE WAY and QuickShield™ and push DOWN AND AWAY using both arms of your QuickShield™ to get to the outside.

Once you have moved your body to a position of advantage, then it is a simple matter of executing Elbow Control #1. In effect you may execute any of the four Elbow Controls, however for purposes of example we will illustrate Elbow Control #1 in conjunction with getting to the outside.

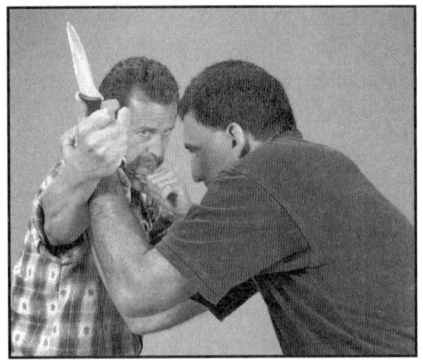

Execute QuickShield™ from the INSIDE position.

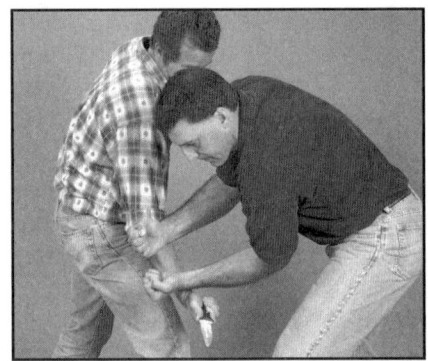

Push down and away and get to the OUTSIDE.

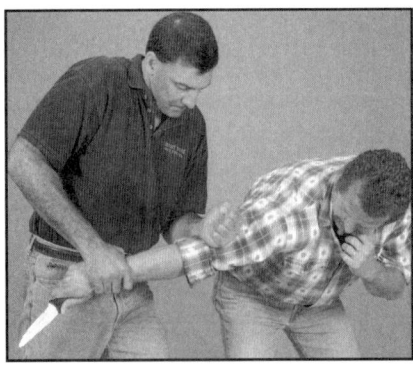

Once you are safely on the OUTSIDE begin to execute Elbow Control #1.

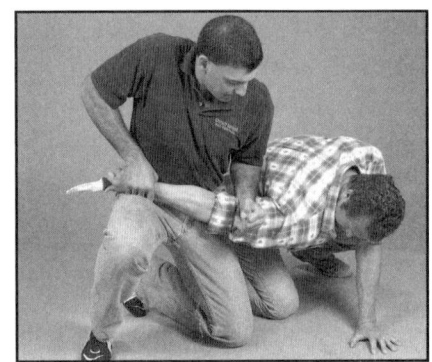

Remember to bring the inside knee down and control his upper body using your weight.

Part Two—Defending Against Non-Contact and Contact Range Attacks

If needed, take him all the way down to a FACE DOWN STABILIZATION using Elbow Control # 2.

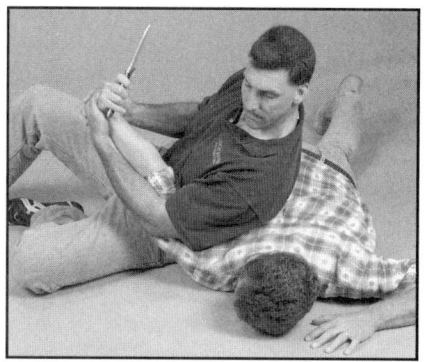

And secure the weapon arm as necessary to your situation.

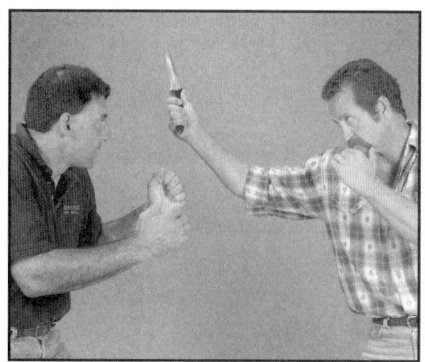

Training partner resets his position and delivers a forehand strike.

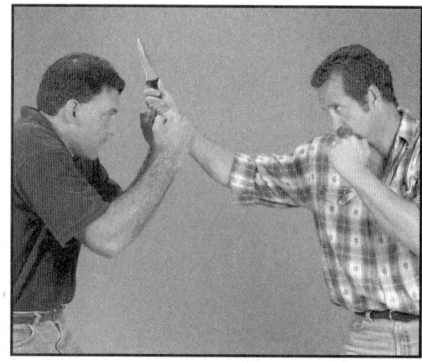

Hands instinctively raise up.

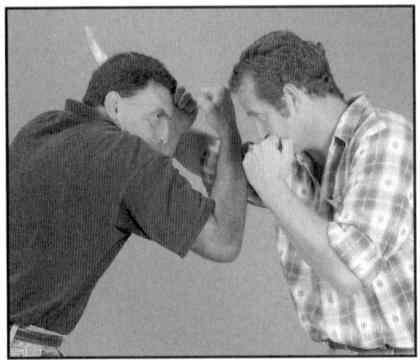

Execute a QuickShield™ defense.

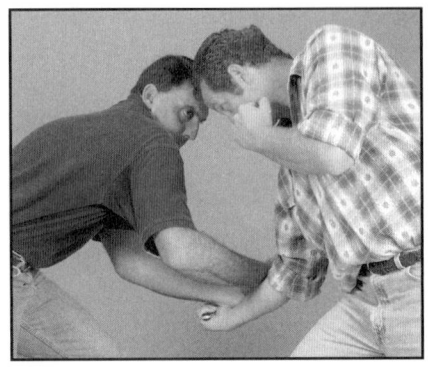

Push DOWN AND AWAY and safely to the OUTSIDE.

In today's modern age of grappling and readily available no-holds-barred training, it should be fairly obvious WHY we don't want to stay on the INSIDE and fight. A good example would be the rear naked choke counter or even a strike to the back of your head with his other hand especially if you turn your back to him. Remember the safest place to be in any altercation is on the OUTSIDE and in a Position of Advantage. This is exactly why we want to push DOWN AND AWAY and get to our Position of Advantage safely to the OUTSIDE.

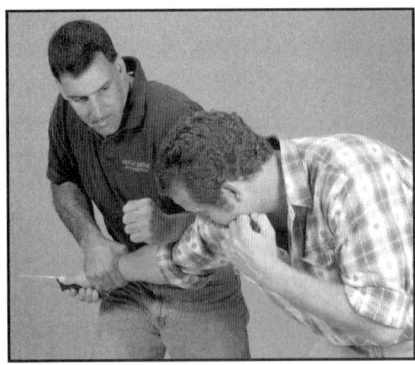

Attempting Elbow Control #1.

He offers resistance and struggles to break free.

Part Two—Defending Against Non-Contact and Contact Range Attacks

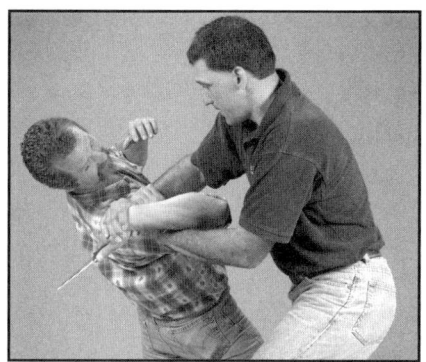

Execute Elbow Control #3

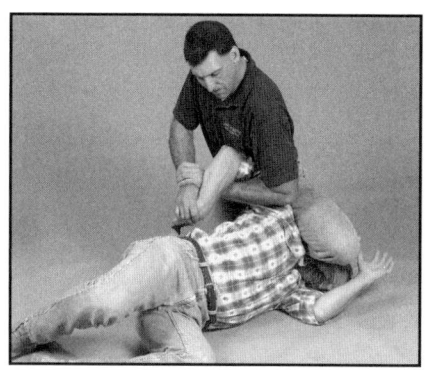

Finish with a FACE UP STABILIZATION.

Much later in your training, once you have mastered the elbow controls you may want to ask your training partners to go at you just a bit more vigorously and then to try and escape to test the validity of your control holds and position. However, even at that time, remember to train safely and with respect to your shoulder and elbow joints.

Advanced Elbow Control Drilling

Training partner gauges for CONTACT RANGE. Starting from ANY position he slowly slashes or thrusts along either the high line or low line with the training blade. Here, you execute and appropriate low line (DOWN AND AWAY) or highline (QuickShield™) basic defense and transition directly into any of the Elbow Controls as we have illustrated above. The remainder of the technique is also the same as above where, once you have successfully secured the weapon arm, you step in with the near foot to take control of his CENTER MASS.

At this stage in the game of training you are equipped with the tools it takes to handle both situations—going in or getting out—applied to both low line and high line attacks. This gives you the tactical edge at both NON-CONTACT and CONTACT RANGES.

Part Three

Defense and Disarming at Extreme Close Quarters

There are three problem areas that must be addressed when problem-solving an edged weapon attack at extreme close quarters:

1. **Rear Obstruction**
2. **Cross-body attack**
3. **No remaining options**

We will address these one at a time.

Rear Obstructions

The typical "What if" scenarios pop up on a regular basis. Often, students will ask "Well, what if..." and the answers are always as ubiquitous as the questions. One example is "What if some guy is sitting in the bushes under the cover of night with a competition rifle about 400 yards away and he shoots at you using advanced optics?" Ok—well not much you can do in that situation. Same thing goes for "What if all of a sudden some guy pops out of the bushes behind you, stabs you right through the heart and takes your wallet?" Again, if you didn't see or hear him and have no forewarning, then this is called an ambush. Although rather unfortunate for the victim, the effectiveness of an ambush is predicated on the fact that reaction is ALWAYS slower than action. If somebody sneaks up behind you with a knife and sticks you with it, then there's really not a whole heck of a lot you can do about it.

One very realistic "What if" that can be encountered in an edged weapon attack is "What if there's something behind you and you can't move backward?" This is what is known as a **REAR OBSTRUCTION**. Simply defined—a scenario where you cannot move backward for whatever reason. Perhaps there's a car, a wall, your wife, another attacker and you cannot move in that direction—what then?

The same technology that is used to BREAK AND CLEAR backward also applies forward, except that you must pass dangerously close to the weapon hand. Since there's no other way around except the way through, there are options available to you should you find yourself caught between an attacker and a REAR OBSTRUCTION at extreme close quarters (ECQ).

Using our basic tools from previous chapters let's begin with the example of a low-line thrust. Forty-five degrees is still the quickest way out, and you still want to BREAK AND CLEAR the CONTACT CONNEC-

PART THREE—DEFENSE AND DISARMING AT ETREME CLOSE QUARTERS

TION and MOVE TO THE OUTSIDE. However, things get a little more difficult when you're traveling near the line of the attack.

First let's take a close look at ECQ footwork.

ECQ Footwork

Step and pivot—what's really going on here?

By employing ECQ (Extreme Close Quarters) footwork you are effectively reducing the size of your attacker's available target (i.e. your body). Additionally, your action is causing him to react thus giving you control over the fight and finally, but most important, you are effectively removing any hindrance caused by REAR OBSTRUCTION (such as a car, wall, family members, wife, girlfriend, etc.)

ELEMENTS OF ECQ FOOTWORK

There are three basic elements of ECQ footwork. These are incorporated in an excellent training drill developed by Puonon Guro Edgar G. Sulite, Founder of the LAMECO system of Eskrima. Known to LAMECO Eskrima International practitioners as "Ha'k ba ng paiwas" or loosely translated "getting out of the way," the essential elements of ECQ footwork are as follows:

Beginning at rest squared off to incoming thread with hands relaxed by your side.

Step up and out 45 degrees (approximately to 10:00 O'clock) while crouching into combative awareness and raising your hands up to center.

Shift your weight to your lead leg and pivot the remainder of your weight on the balls of your lead foot quickly bringing your center mass instantly off the line of attack.

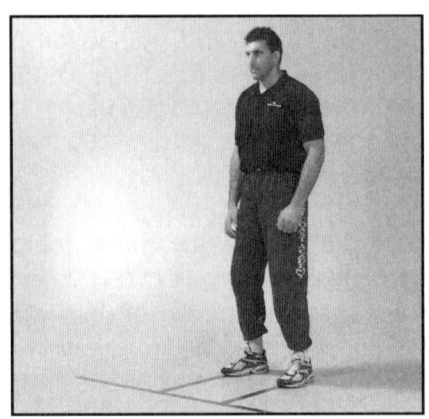

Reset to your original position at rest squared off to incoming thread with hands relaxed by your side.

Step up and out 45 degrees in the other direction (approximately to 2:00 O'clock) while crouching into combative awareness and raising your hands up to center.

Again shift your weight to your lead leg and pivot the remainder of your weight on the balls of your lead foot quickly bringing your center mass instantly off the line of attack while staying focused and keeping your eyes on the threat.

Part Three—Defense and Disarming at Etreme Close Quarters

Throughout my years of training up in Stockton with Grandmaster Giron, Master Tony Somera, Guro Dexter Labonog, Guro Glenn Abrescy and the Bahla Na Group, it was very difficult to keep alignment of toes, knee and chin while in motion and under tremendous pressure (attacks from these teachers is powerful and lighting fast). So to help out the beginning students, they came up with a great mnemonic to remember this crucial TOE-KNEE-CHIN alignment for ECQ evasion footwork. They called it "Tony Chin—a good Chinese friend of mine—he helps me win fights!"

Alignment of the toe, knee and chin for maximum speed in the pivot.

ECQ Footwork Drill #1

Passed down to us from Punong Guro Edgar G. Sulite—the "Ha'k ba ng paiwas" drill.

Stand with your back to a wall. Your training partner is standing facing you and the wall. Ask your training partner to gauge for ECQ distance. Training partner thrusts toward your CENTER MASS about belt level with training implement. Execute step and pivot to the outside. Step back to center. Training partner resets and then thrusts again for the exact same spot. You then step and pivot to the opposite side. Your training partner resets again and you begin the drill again from the top.

The Naked Edge: The Complete Guide to Edged Weapons Defense

Stand with your back to the wall. Your training partner is standing facing you and the wall.

Your training partner delivers a slow and controlled thrusts towards your CENTER MASS about belt level with training knife. You're immediate reaction is to raise your hands, begin to turn and crouch down (to reduce target size)and step off to 45 degrees from the line of attack.

Training partner continues thrusting forward to ensure that you have moved safely to the outside and have successfully completed your ECQ evasion footwork.

Part Three—Defense and Disarming at Extreme Close Quarters

Your training partner resets again and you begin the drill again from the top.

Your partner thrusts to your center as before and this time you step to the other side up 45 degrees off the line of attack.

Complete your pivot and get to his outside.

ECQ Handwork

Closing the car door or smashing the forearm are your best options at ECQ range. You always want to keep the second hand free to CONTROL THE ELBOW.

There are three options available for ECQ Handwork:
1. Closing the car door—which we already covered—using the palm.
2. Slamming the car door—using the forearm—DOWN AND AWAY.
3. Classic Filipino outside vertical scissor-hands (gunting) outside pass.

Closing the Car Door (review from previous chapters)

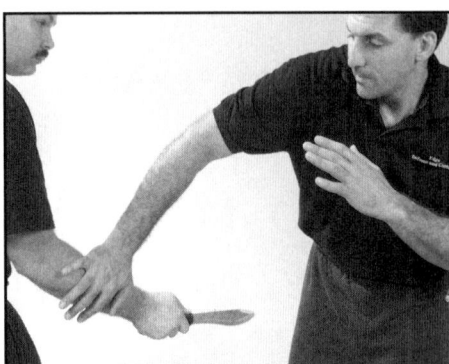

Closing the car door—palm down and away.

Slamming the Car Door (Indonesian—Cimande method)

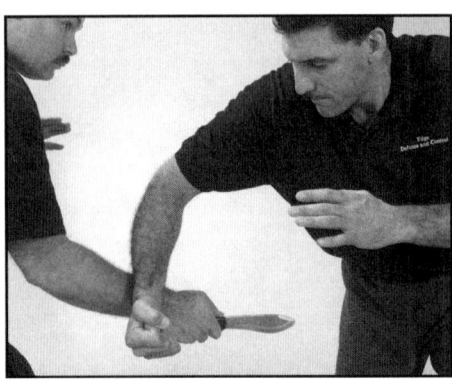

Slamming the car door—forearm down and away.

PART THREE—DEFENSE AND DISARMING AT EXTREME CLOSE QUARTERS

Outside Pass (Gunting—classic Filipino method)

 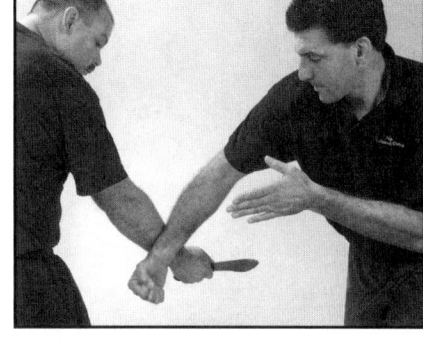

Initial move—palm down and away.   *Final move—forearm down and away.*

These ECQ handwork options are like clothing—some will fit your body type perfectly while others may be as foreign to you as having eleven fingers. To quote my instructor Guro Dan Inosanto—"Take what is useful to your body type and personality."

ECQ Handwork Drill #1

From Frozen Foot only, training partner gauges for ECQ distance and then delivers a slow and controlled thrust to your midsection. Your response is to **CLOSE THE CAR DOOR** while simultaneously executing ECQ FOOTWORK DRILL #1.

Your training partner gauges with you for ECQ rage and delivers a slow and controlled thrust to your mid-section.

Execute ECQ Footwork Drill #1 while simultaneously applying CLOSE THE CAR DOOR.

Complete your pivot (remember "Tony Chin") and get to his outside.

In this next sequence (which is part of the same drill), same exact ECQ footwork but this time, substitute CLOSE THE CAR DOOR with SLAM THE CAR DOOR.

From "Frozen Foot," training partner gauges for ECQ distance and then delivers a slow and controlled thrust to your midsection. Your response is to SLAM THE CAR DOOR while simultaneously executing ECQ FOOTWORK DRILL #1 and move safely to his outside.

PART THREE—DEFENSE AND DISARMING AT EXTREME CLOSE QUARTERS

In this next sequence (also part of this same drill) again, same exact ECQ footwork but substitute SLAM THE CAR DOOR with the classic Filipino OUTSIDE PASS (outside vertical gunting).

From "Frozen Foot," training partner gauges for ECQ distance and then delivers a slow and controlled thrust to your midsection. Your response is now OUTSIDE PASS while simultaneously executing ECQ FOOTWORK DRILL #1 and move safely to his outside.

Now that you've effectively handled the barrier of a rear obstruction using any of the above combination ECQ handwork and footwork combinations, you are now free to BREAK AND CLEAR and MOVE TO THE OUTSIDE. However, there may be the factor of the attacker's recovery speed where you need to employ just one more element of personal safety.

Safety Hand

The safety hand, (some people call it the CHECK HAND) plays an integral role in CONTROLLING THE ELBOW at ECQ ranges.

The primary reason why we employ the opposite hand to execute either CLOSE THE CAR DOOR, SLAM THE CAR DOOR ort the OUTSIDE PASS is to keep the SAFETY or CHECK HAND free and available for immediate usage.

The "C"-Clamp—Grandmaster Leo M. Giron

The importance of the "c-clamp" as taught to me by Grandmaster Leo M. Giron—Founder of the Bahala Na system of Escrima—is to secure and CONTROL THE ATTACKING ELBOW following whatever options you choose to exercise.

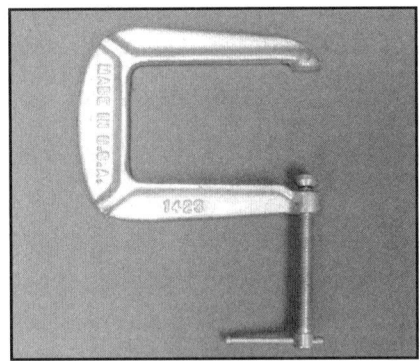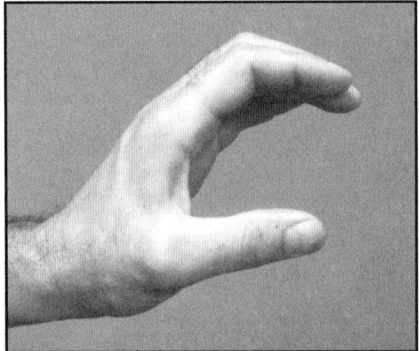

Grandmaster Giron's "C-CLAMP" originated from the carpenters' "c"-clamp, which is used to hold something in place while you work on it. The same concept applies to your empty hand defense as part of ECQ handwork.

Part Three—Defense and Disarming at Etreme Close Quarters

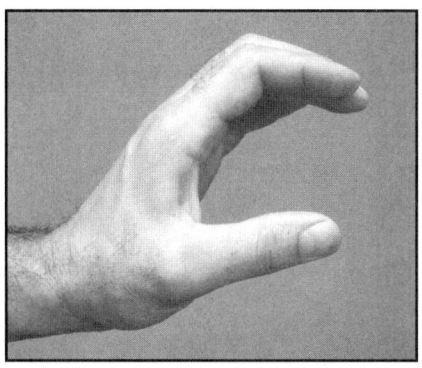 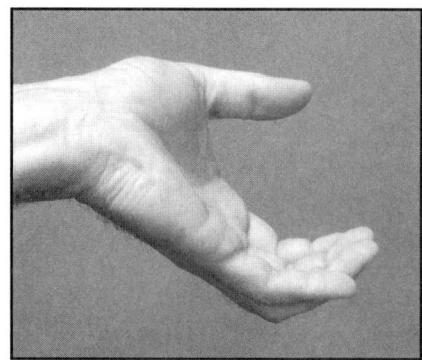

Examples of practical application of the Giron C-CLAMP can be with the palm facing downward or the palm facing upward.

The concept of the "C-clamp" is that if he's sweaty, bloody, or just moving way to fast, you can't take the chance of your check hand slipping off his elbow at this range. In other words if you try to control a slippery forearm or triceps without the use of your opposing digit, it would be nearly impossible for your safety hand to provide any significant control of the attacking weapon arm. However, with the employment of your thumb with either palm facing downward or palm facing upward (Grandmaster Giron is a proponent of palm facing upward for maximum efficiency) you can better control his elbow and thus control his attacking motion.

ECQ Handwork Drill #2
Training partner gauges for ECQ distance and then delivers a slow and controlled thrust to your midsection. Your response is CLOSE THE CAR DOOR while simultaneously executing ECQ FOOTWORK DRILL #1, then apply the check hand using the c-clamp, BREAK AND CLEAR to SAFETY RANGE, MOVE TO THE OUTSIDE, then LOOK AND ASSES.

Handling the Rear Obstruction at ECQ range:
1. ECQ handwork (CLOSE THE CAR DOOR) plus ECQ footwork
2. Check/ safety hand using C-clamp
3. BREAK AND CLEAR while Move to the outside
4. LOOK AND ASSESS

The Naked Edge: The Complete Guide to Edged Weapons Defense

Gauge with your partner for ECQ range. He delivers a slow and controlled thrust to your mid-section.

Execute ECQ handwork CLOSING THE CAR DOOR plus ECQ FOOTWORK DRILL #1.

Apply the check hand using the C-CLAMP.

BREAK AND CLEAR to SAFETY RANGE, MOVE TO THE OUTSIDE, then LOOK AND ASSESS.

Part Three—Defense and Disarming at Extreme Close Quarters

ECQ Handwork Drill #3

Training partner resets to center, gauges for ECQ distance and then delivers a slow and controlled thrust to your midsection. Your response is SLAM THE CAR DOOR while simultaneously executing ECQ FOOTWORK DRILL #1, then apply the check hand using the c-clamp, BREAK AND CLEAR to SAFETY RANGE, MOVE TO THE OUTSIDE, then LOOK AND ASSES.

Handling the Rear Obstruction at ECQ range:
1. SLAM THE CAR door using ECQ footwork
2. Check/ safety hand using C-clamp
3. BREAK AND CLEAR while Move to the outside
4. LOOK AND ASSESS

Gauge with your partner for ECQ range. He delivers a slow and controlled thrust to your mid-section.

Execute ECQ handwork SLAM THE CAR DOOR plus ECQ FOOTWORK DRILL #1.

Apply the check hand using the C-CLAMP.

The Naked Edge: The Complete Guide to Edged Weapons Defense

*BREAK AND CLEAR to SAFETY RANGE,
MOVE TO THE OUTSIDE, then LOOK AND ASSESS.*

ECQ Handwork Drill #4

Training partner resets to center, gauges for ECQ distance and then delivers a slow and controlled thrust to your midsection. Your response is OUTSIDE PASS while simultaneously executing ECQ FOOTWORK DRILL #1, then apply the check hand using the c-clamp, BREAK AND CLEAR to SAFETY RANGE, MOVE TO THE OUTSIDE, then look and asses.

Handling the Rear Obstruction at ECQ range:
1. OUTSIDE PASS using ECQ footwork
2. Check/ safety hand using C-clamp
3. BREAK AND CLEAR while Move to the outside
4. LOOK AND ASSESS

Gauge with your partner for ECQ range. He delivers a slow and controlled thrust to your mid-section.

Part Three—Defense and Disarming at Etreme Close Quarters

Execute ECQ handwork OUTSIDE PASS plus ECQ FOOTWORK DRILL #1.

Apply the check hand using the C-CLAMP. Remember to complete your full pivot to the outside using "Tony Chin."

BREAK AND CLEAR to SAFETY RANGE, MOVE TO THE OUTSIDE, then LOOK AND ASSESS.

An Important Note About "Getting Out" and "Going In"

Although getting away from an edged weapon attack—especially if you have nothing in your hands with which to defend yourself—is your best option, in certain street scenarios you may find yourself in a situation where you may need to "go in." This may either be by choice or just happen to be where you end up in an altercation.

Having covered our "Getting out" or "disengage" section of ECQ handwork and footwork, now let's take a look at our "Get in" or "engage" options.

ECQ Handwork Drill #5

Training partner gauges for ECQ distance and then delivers a slow and controlled thrust to your midsection. Your response can be either of the three ECQ Handworks while simultaneously executing ECQ FOOTWORK DRILL #1, then apply the check hand using the c-clamp, UNDER/ OVER and follow-up.

Handling the Rear Obstruction at ECQ range:
1. ECQ Handwork using ECQ footwork
2. Check/ safety hand using C-clamp
3. UNDER/ OVER to follow-up

Starting at ECQ range, your partner thrusts to your mid-section, you execute any of the ECQ handworks plus the ECQ footwork pivot and C-CLAMP safety hand. Then, for whatever reason, it is necessary for you to step in and execute an UNDER/OVER elbow control lock and takedown.

Part Three—Defense and Disarming at Extreme Close Quarters

ECQ Handwork Drill #6

Training partner resets to center and then gauges for ECQ distance and then delivers a slow and controlled thrust to your midsection. Your response can be either of the three ECQ Handworks while simultaneously executing ECQ FOOTWORK DRILL #1, then apply the check hand using the c-clamp, Elbow Control # 1 (Velcro Arm Bar) and follow-up.

Handling the Rear Obstruction at ECQ range:
1. ECQ Handwork using ECQ footwork.
2. Check/safety hand using C-clamp.
3. Elbow Control # 1 (Velcro Arm Bar) to follow-up.

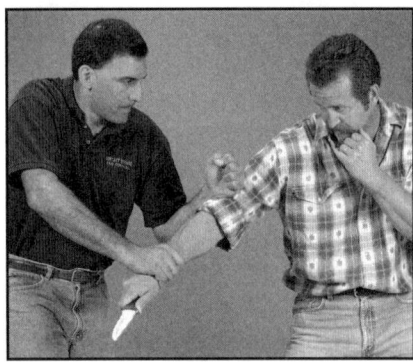
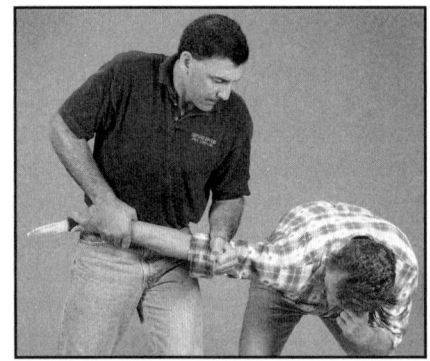

Starting at ECQ range, your partner thrusts to your mid-section, you execute any of the ECQ handworks plus the ECQ footwork pivot and C-CLAMP safety hand, but the C-CLAMP slips off upward and for whatever reason, it is necessary for you to close in and execute an elbow control lock and takedown.

Part Three—Defense and Disarming at Extreme Close Quarters

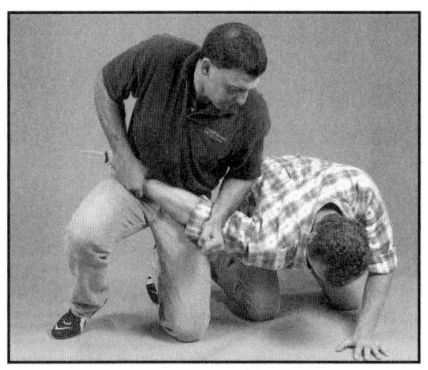
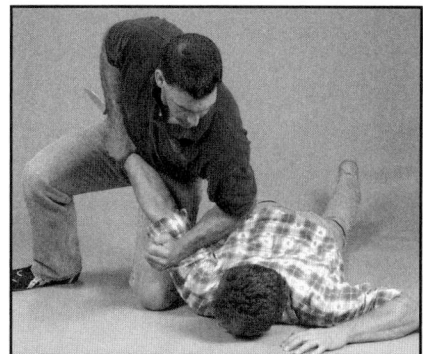
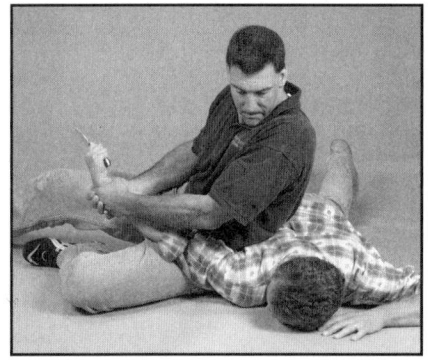
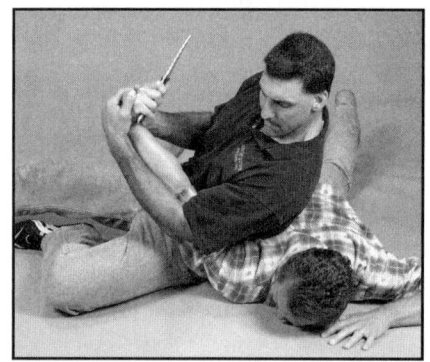

Cross-Body

Up to now we have analyzed optimum response for escapes to the outside and even escapes in the event of a rear obstruction. But, what if you can't get to the outside to execute any of the ECQ Handworks?

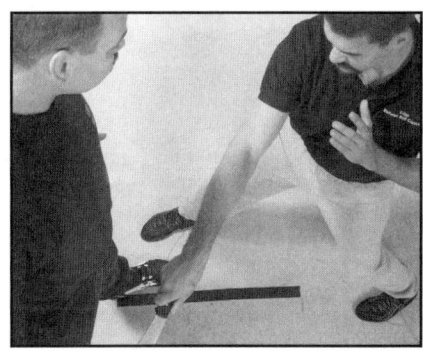
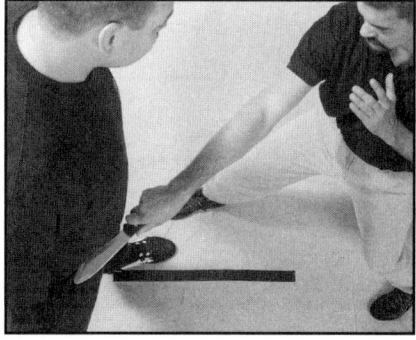

Example of cross-body positioning whereas it is just about impossible to employ standard ECQ handwork and ECQ footwork to get to the outside and either "Get Out" or "Get In."

In the event that you are cut off from the outside (which means that your stuck on the inside and must pass through the on-line and outside positions), this is known as a CROSS BODY CONDITION. The best way to handle cross-body conditions is to execute an optimum Cross-Body maneuver.

The safest and most effective way to handle any cross-body condition is to employ the SLAM THE CAR DOOR plus DOWN AND AWAY. This is what I call a "FEED RAMP" named after part of the mechanism for feeding cartridges from magazine storage and into battery in firearms.

Cross Body Drill #1 (feed ramp)

To get a feel for how a FEED RAMP works, first gauge with your partner for ECQ range, then try alternate strike positions employing the back of your forearms. Remember that we offer the back of the forearm in the vent of getting cut at least it's a bit less damage that on the inside of the forearms.

Gauge with your training partner for ECQ range.

PART THREE—DEFENSE AND DISARMING AT ETREME CLOSE QUARTERS

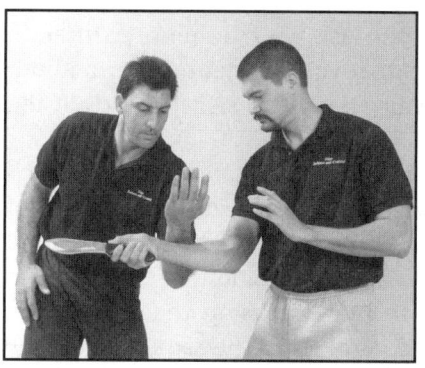

Employ FEED RAMP against incoming low-line thrust and push down and away from your body ensuring distance from the edge and tip.

Employ FEED RAMP against incoming high-line slash and push down and away from your body ensuring distance from the edge and tip.

Now try switching arms and using a FEED RAMP against incoming high-line slash and push down and away from your body ensuring distance from the edge and tip.

Now try switching arms again and using a FEED RAMP against incoming low-line slash and push down and away from your body ensuring distance from the edge and tip.

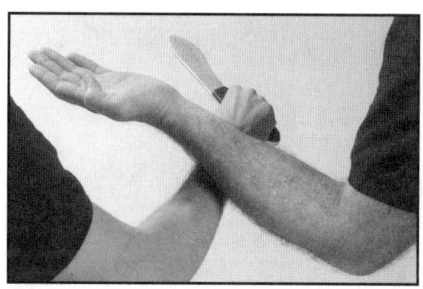

Now try switching arms again and ask your training partner to switch arms. Again employ a FEED RAMP against incoming low-line slash and push down and away from your body ensuring distance from the edge and tip.

Repeat this several times and then ask your training partner to switch hands every once and a while so that you can get training on both sides. Remember that you can't ask your attacker to switch hands in the middle of the street!

Now let's put all the pieces together. Using the same training principles as established earlier, there are two options in solving the problem of escaping an ECQ edged weapon altercation—either "get out" (break and clear the contact connection and get to superior position) or "Get in" and immobilize that attacking weapon arm by controlling the elbow with either a safety hand and/or an elbow control lock. The same technology applies to a cross-body condition.

Cross Body Drill #2 (getting out)

This section provides optimum training to get to the outside and BREAK AND CLEAR from either a high or low line attack. This drill should be executed at slow speeds until you feel comfortable enough to increase the pace.

Ask your training partner to gauge for ECQ range. Stand slightly to the inside to establish a cross-body escape scenario.

Training partner then delivers a slow and controlled low line thrust to your mid-section. Use the FEED RAMP to deflect the incoming thrust.

Part Three—Defense and Disarming at Etreme Close Quarters

Push down and away to ensure safe distance from edge/ point and your body.

Now execute ECQ footwork and ECQ handwork, BREAK AND CLEAR, LOOK AND ASSESS.

Your partner now resets to center and prepares to deliver a highline backhand slash from the high closed position. Ask your training partner to gauge for ECQ range. Stand slightly to the inside to establish a cross-body escape scenario.

Training partner delivers a slow and controlled high-line backhand slash.

The Naked Edge: The Complete Guide to Edged Weapons Defense

Use the FEED RAMP to deflect the incoming thrust.

Push down and away to ensure safe distance from edge/ point and your body.

Now execute ECQ footwork and ECQ handwork, BREAK AND CLEAR, LOOK AND ASSESS.

Cross Body Drill #3 (getting in)

This section provides optimum training to get to the outside and use any elbow control from either a high or low line attack. This drill should be executed at slow speeds until you feel comfortable enough to increase the pace.

Before training in this drill you it is important to have trained enough repetitions in the elbow control drills.

Part Three— Defense and Disarming at Etreme Close Quarters

Ask your training partner to gauge for ECQ range. Stand slightly to the inside to establish a cross-body escape scenario.

Training partner then delivers a slow and controlled low line thrust to your mid-section. Use the FEED RAMP to deflect the incoming thrust.

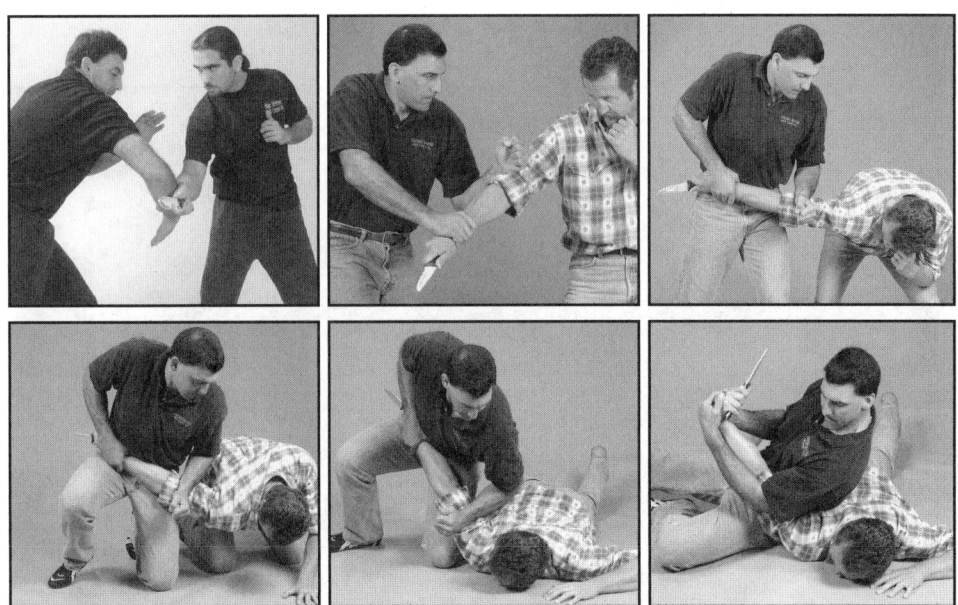

Now execute ECQ footwork, and engage ("Get In") using any elbow Control to takedown.

The Naked Edge: The Complete Guide to Edged Weapons Defense

Reset back to center squared off to your training partner. Ask your training partner to gauge for ECQ range. Stand slightly to the inside to establish a cross-body escape scenario.

Training partner then delivers a slow and controlled low line thrust to your mid-section. Use the FEED RAMP to deflect the incoming thrust.

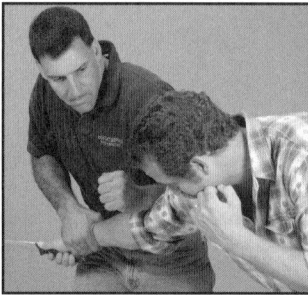

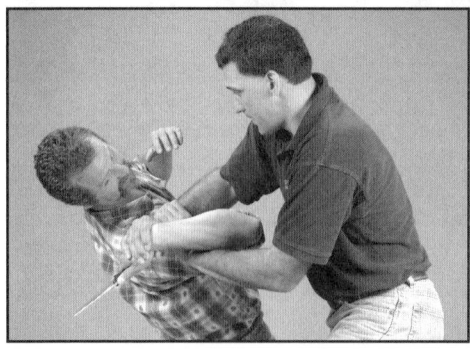

Now execute ECQ footwork, and engage ("Get In") using any elbow control to takedown.

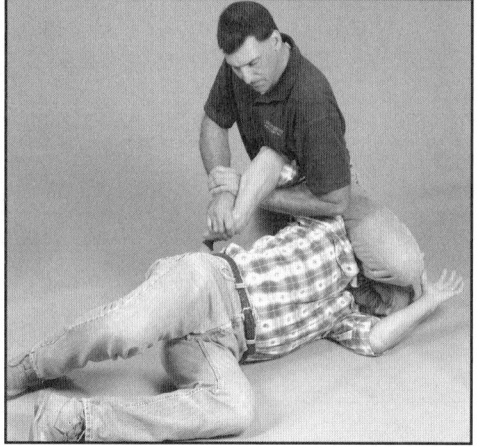

Part Three—Defense and Disarming at Etreme Close Quarters

Again the keys to these drills are repetition. The best way to get really good at anything is to do it over and over again.

"Steve, you must do one thousand times."
—Punong Guro Edgar G. Sulite

An interesting side note to the "magic" of repetitions is that modern researchers have found that the first one thousand repetitions imprints a neuropsychological pathway. The second thousand reps widens that neuropsychological pathway and the third thousand reps converts a neuropsychological pathway and its sympathetic musculature actions into subconscious reactive response.

Disarms—No Remaining Options

The third and final problem area regarding edged weapon attacks at ECQ range we discussed earlier was NO REMAINING OPTIONS. This is the ugliest and most unforgiving of all ECQ and for that matter any edged weapon attack. This is where it's "do or die trying"—your last ditch effort.

The best disarms are those executed either by accident or by incident. Similar to walking into the side of a desk or a doorknob with something in your hand and that something pops out of your hand as a result of the impact—they just so happen to occur—by accident.

Disarms are reserved for those times when there is no other option available.

There are two key principles regarding disarming:
1. Control of the opposing digit (thumb)
2. Control of the direction of force

Father of the Four Fingers

Punong Guro Edgar G. Sulite—one of the top edged weapons practitioners and master level instructors of this modern age espoused a very important concept when teaching disarming of an edged weapon.

"Steve, the thumb is the father of the four fingers."
—Punong Guro Edgar G. Sulite

The Naked Edge: The Complete Guide to Edged Weapons Defense

No truer words have ever been spoken regarding training in the skills of disarming. The opposing digit is what we humans employ to hold anything in our grasp. If the opposing digit is compromised then by default so is the contact connection.

Hand-in-hand with the sage advice of Punong Guro Sulite is DO NOT GRAB THE WRIST. If you grab the wrist then his hand is still free to move and even more importantly the thumb (father of the four fingers) is still in control of the contact connection. Should you chose to take control of the contact connection (at the point of the attacker's grip) then you must control his opposing digit.

Capturing the thumb—father of the four fingers:

Incorrect grasp of the base of the thumb—notice that all four fingers are not firmly wrapped around the attacker's thumb.

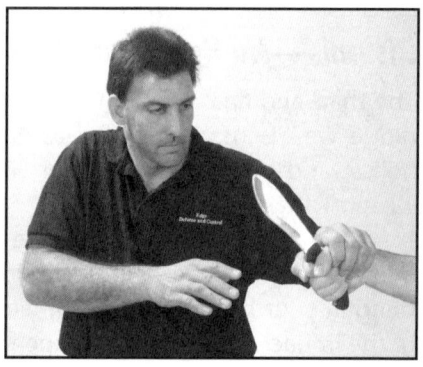

Correct grasp of the base of the attacker's thumb. Your four fingers are now in control of the attacker's opposing digit and thus are in control of that part of the contact connection.

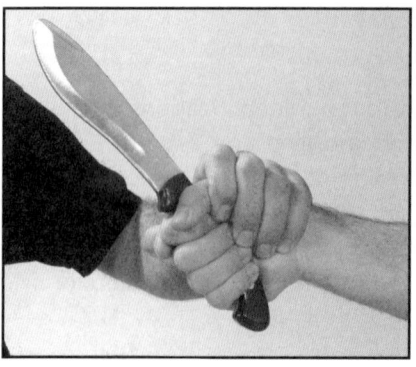

Close-up of proper placement of four fingers base of the thumb.

PART THREE—DEFENSE AND DISARMING AT ETREME CLOSE QUARTERS

Meeting and Following

There are two additionally important elements of disarming which are handed down to us by both Grandmaster Leo M. Giron and Guro Dan Inosanto. These are the force vectors "Meet" and "Follow."

If a strike is moving toward us and we meet that strike with equal and opposing force with a strike of our own, then this is an example of force against force or force meeting force or simply "meet."

If a strike is moving toward us and we pass behind that strike applying force behind it such as using your body to push a stalled car up a hill, then this is an example of force following force or simply "follow."

Just so that we're all on the same page these terms "meet" and "follow" will be used to describe force vectors in application to disarming techniques.

Classical Disarming of an Edged Weapon

Classical disarm of any style grip or attack to can result in either one of two desirable conditions:

A "strip"—where an edged weapon is simply stripped from the attackers grip.

A "takeaway"—where you take the edged weapon away from the attacker and now hold it in your grasp to employ as you deem appropriate.

Reverse Grip Inside Disarm

In this scenario you are taken by surprise by a reverse grip thrust to your throat above the clavicle (your collar bone). It is happening too fast and as a complete surprise and you are not in a position to execute either ECQ footwork or ECQ handwork to escape. In other words, you're up against the wall and there's nothing else you can do—you've got NO REMAINING OPTIONS.

In this example here is an optimum solution.

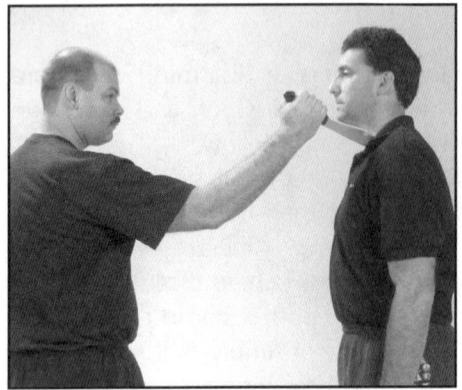

Training Partner Assumes reverse grip and gauges for ECQ range to primary target.

Training partner delivers a slow and controlled forehand thrusts to just above your clavicle toward the primary target area.

Simultaneously attack the opponent's throat or eyes with your far hand as the near hand grasps his wrist and up tight against the flat of the blade. Your wrist bone should be locked tight so as to immobilize the movement of the knife.

Part Three—Defense and Disarming at Etreme Close Quarters

Bring your locked arm straight down (do not pull into yourself) and turn his hand into your centerline.

Take your free hand and turn it palm up grasping the base of his thumb with your four fingers effectively immobilizing his attack hand.

Take full control of his weapon arm by increasing the torque using his thumb.

Start to slide down his forearm (stay attached and DO NOT lift your hand) maintaining control by his thumb.

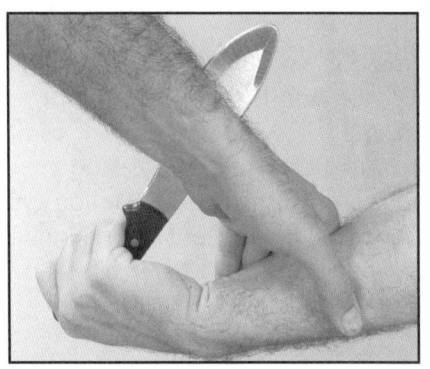

Incorrect position for takeaway which may result in a laceration—especially with a double edge or of the edge is facing backward.

The Naked Edge: The Complete Guide to Edged Weapons Defense

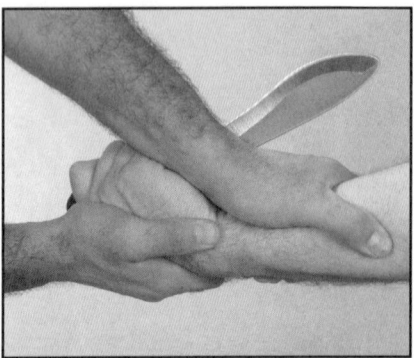

Correct position for takeaway—stay connected to the forearm.

Keeping the connection to his forearm continue to slide down and away from your body until you now have the knife in your own grasp by the handle resulting in a successful takeaway.

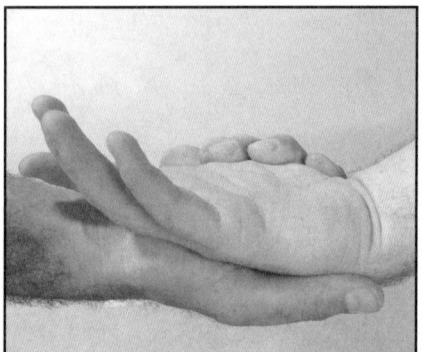

Continue to maintain influence of his upper body with the thumb control—maintaining a firm grip with your four fingers on the base of his thumb.

Reverse Grip Inside Disarm Option

In some cases, a trained knife fighter may be sensitive enough to feel a disarm in progress. A realistic "what if " scenario is that you attempt to apply the takeaway as in the previous example however he senses it coming and powers through your attempt thus succeeding in breaking your grip ending up in the palm down position. Again, he is too close for you to evade using ECQ footwork or ECQ handwork or even put something in between yourself and the blade. Again you've got no where to go and nothing you can do—you've got NO REMAINING OPTIONS.

PART THREE—DEFENSE AND DISARMING AT ETREME CLOSE QUARTERS

Training Partner Assumes reverse grip, gauges for ECQ range on primary target and delivers a slow and controlled forehand thrust just to above your clavicle. Here you attempt to execute the previous disarm. However, he's on to your attempt and abruptly turns his hand over in order to prevent himself from being stripped.

The Naked Edge: The Complete Guide to Edged Weapons Defense

Keep your free hand up and in your center. Allow him to push just past your centerline.

Drop your free hand straight down over his thumb position and direct the bone of your left arm in the opposite direction of your pushing right hand. This results in extreme pressure against his thumb and causes the handle of the knife to loosen and eventually evacuate his grip.

Similar to the action of wringing out a wet towel, move both your forearms with equal and opposing force eliminating the space between your forearm and the flat of the blade as well as significantly increasing the pressure on his weakening grip.

Continue with opposing pressure until the knife flies from his grasp resulting in a successful strip.

Closing the Car Door Disarm (Forearm Strip)

Training partner assumes a SABER or HAMMER grip (tip forward) and gauges for ECQ range.

Training then delivers a slow and controlled thrust to your mid-section at about belt level.

Using CLOSING THE CAR DOOR continue to push DOWN AND AWAY until the knife is safely past your CENTERLINE.

Take your support hand and go PALM DOWN into a C-CLAMP around the meatiest portion of his thumb. Your fingers should be pointing inward.

The Naked Edge: The Complete Guide to Edged Weapons Defense

Grab his thumb and forcefully pull it down and away from you. At this time your forearm should be pushing DOWN AND AWAY against the flat of the blade in the opposite direction.

Four fingers base of his thumb push into the weakest part of his grip immobilizing the flat of the blade against the safest part of your forearm should you get cut.

Continue pushing with your forearm as you forcefully pop the knife out of his grasp with your four fingers gripping hand resulting in a successful strip.

Part Three—Defense and Disarming at Extreme Close Quarters

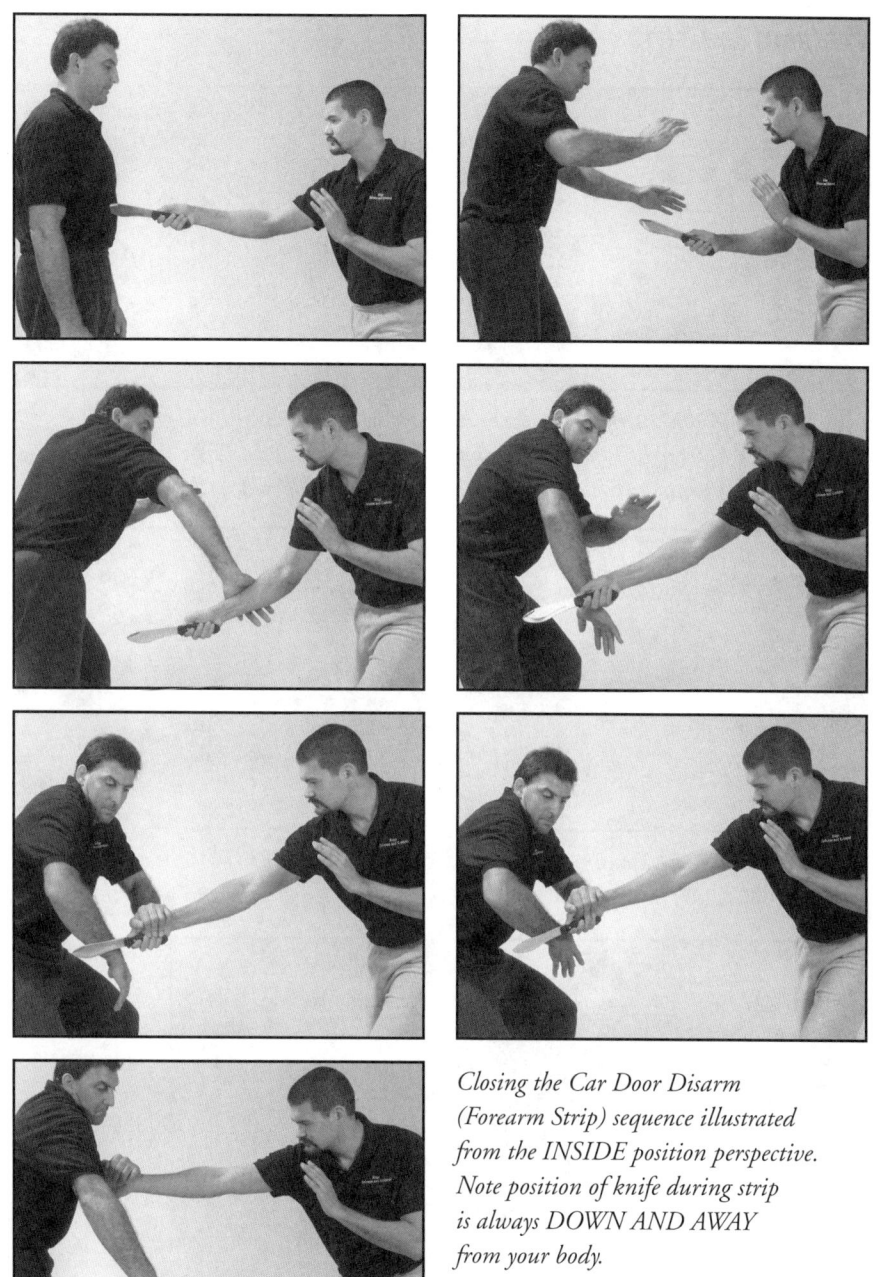

Closing the Car Door Disarm (Forearm Strip) sequence illustrated from the INSIDE position perspective. Note position of knife during strip is always DOWN AND AWAY from your body.

C-Clamp Leg Strip

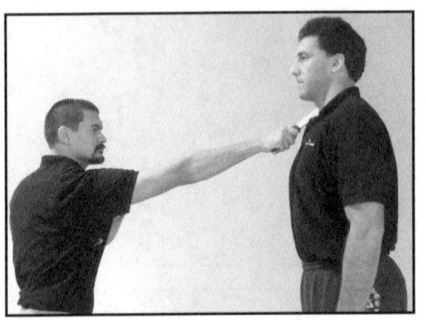

Training Partner Assumes either a HAMMER or a SABER grip, gauges for ECQ range for primary target and then delivers a slow and controlled backhand slash to the side of your neck.

Execute a MEET technique (QuickShield™) plus an ELBOW CONTROL using C-CLAMP while sliding attached hand down toward the base of his thumb.

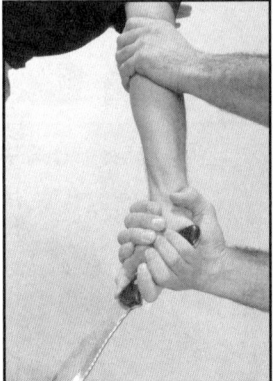

Continue fluid motion down and away from your body.

Attached hand slides down to assume four-finger control of his thumb while the C-CLAMP locks down maintaining elbow control.

PART THREE—DEFENSE AND DISARMING AT EXTREME CLOSE QUARTERS

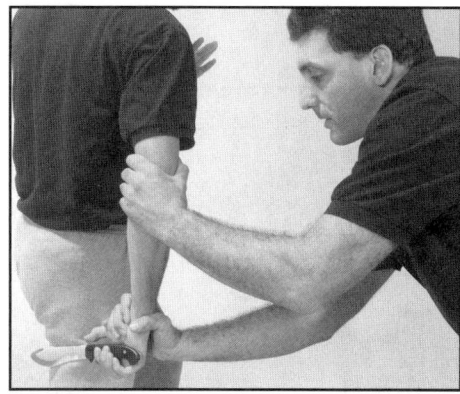

Suddenly reverse your motion in the opposite direction as you hook his leg with his own blade. Maintain that death-grip of his elbow with your C-CLAMP elbow control.

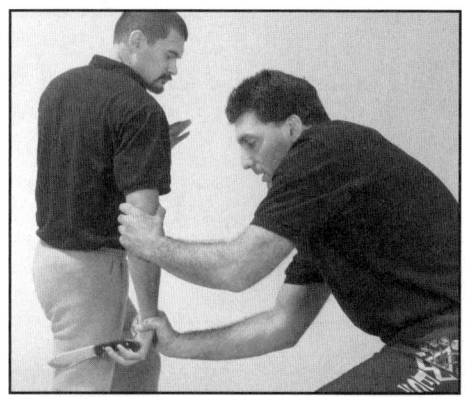

Continue to apply pressure to the back of his leg using both hands and start to build torque with your four-fingers grip hand against the back of his leg.

Abruptly twist your four-fingers grip hand and push forcefully on his elbow thus stripping it out of his hand resulting in a successful strip.

Cross Body Feed Ramp Strip

Training Partner Assumes either a HAMMER or a SABER grip and gauges for ECQ range focusing on primary target.

Training partner delivers a slow and controlled backhand slash to your neck. Immediately execute an QuickShield™ movement. Your support hand comes down and grabs as close as possible to the wrist joint as your contact forearm pushes DOWN AND AWAY.

Using your check hand, slide down his forearm four finger assume fast control of the base of his weapon thumb. Simultaneously position your forearm safely against the flat or back of the blade. Forcefully turn his wrist PALM UP and DOWN AND AWAY as your right forearm moves from his forearm to the flat of his blade.

PART THREE—DEFENSE AND DISARMING AT ETREME CLOSE QUARTERS

Exert opposing forces thus stripping the blade away from his hand from the inside position resulting in a successful strip.

There are literally hundreds of disarms—some more elaborate than others. Once you've mastered the basics the secret of the universe—as you've probably already heard—is repetitions.

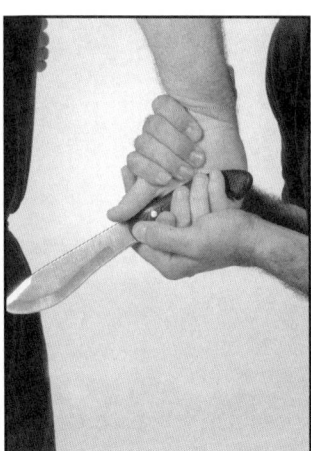 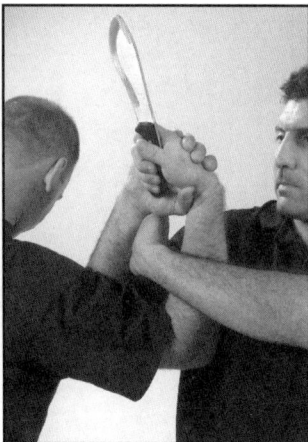 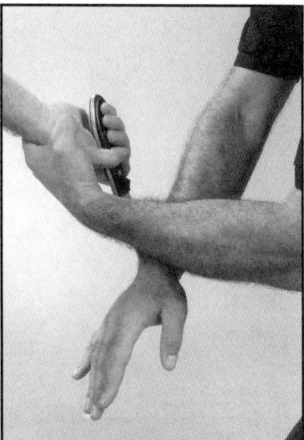

Bibliography

Amberger, Christopher J., *The Secret History of the Sword*, Hammerterz Forum, Germany, 1996

Bull, Stephen, *An Historical Guide to Arms and Armor*, Facts on File.

Clemens, John, *Renaissance Swordmanship—The Illustrated Use of Rapiers and Cut-and-Thrust Swords*, Paladin Press, Colorado, 1997

Diagram Group, *WEAPONS*, St Martin's Press, New York, 1980

Diderot et D'alembert, *L'encylopedie; Recueuil de planches sur les sciences, les arts liberaux et les mechaniques avec leur explications*, France, date of publication unknown.

Evangelista, Nick, *The Encyclopedia of the Sword*, Greenwood Press, London, 1995

Hergpell, Gustav, *Talhoffers Fecht Buch*, Germany, 1462

Inosanto, Dan, *The Filipino Martial Arts*, Know Now Pub. Co., LA, 1980

Levine, Bernard, *Levines Guide to Knives & Their Values*, DNI Books Inc, 1985

Levine, Bernard, *Pocket Knives*, Courage Books, 1993

Newark, Tim, *The Barbarians—Warriors, Weapons and Warefare of the Dark Ages*, Blandford Press, London, 1985

Oakeshott, R. Ewart, *The Archeology of Weapons*, New York, 1996

Penguin, *Encyclopedia of Weapons*, Penguin, date of publication unknown.

Peterson, Daniel, *The Roman Legions*, Crowood Press Ltd., Wiltshire, England, 1992

Peterson, Harold L., *American Knives*, Charles Scribners Sons, New York, 1958

Silver, Sir George, *Paradoxes of Defense*, London, 1599

Strung, Norma M., *An Encyclopedia of Knives*, J.B. Lippincott Co.

Sulite, Edgar G., *The Masters of Arnis, Kali & Eskrima*, Socorro Publishing Company, Philippines, 1993

Turner, Craig and Soper, Tony, *Methods and Practice of Elizabethan Swordplay*, Southern Illinois University Press, 1990

Wilkinson, Frederick, *Arms and Armour*, Hamlyn, London, 1978

Contact Weapons Street Survival Formula

The four steps listed below are the keys to surviving a contact weapon attack at long range. Each time you drill you should make sure that these elements are present and applied with great attention to detail. Additionally, only after sufficient repetitions will the actions be ingrained as second nature.

1. **BREAK CONTACT CONNECTION**
2. **CLEAR TO SAFETY RANGE**
3. **ESTABLISH SUPERIOR POSITION**
4. **LOOK AND ASSESS**

Defending Against Non-Contact Range Attacks

When defending against a contact weapon it is the CONTACT CONNECTION, which must be controlled at all costs.

If you're already at Non-Contact Range, then why close in and place yourself at higher risk?

In situations where an attacker may be at Contact or Extreme Close Quarters (ECQ) range, there is usually not enough time to react using only footwork to break the CONTACT CONNECTION and clear to safety range. Thus, it becomes necessary to assist your footwork with optimum upper body reactive response.

Security and law enforcement personnel generally comment; "Well, if he's moving at me with a knife or something in his hand, then I'll just blast him with my…" The problem is that at close or ECQ range a contact weapon is already on its way *before you even start* to reach for your firearm, baton, or OC spray, or even to use your feet to get off the line of attack. *Reaction is always slower than action.*

Street Survival Table

Response	Stage	Control Method	Range
GET OUT	Stage 1	Footwork	Non-contact/Contact
	Stage 2	Hands and Footwork	Contact/ECQ
GET IN	Stage 3	Elbow Control	ECQ

Additionally, I'd like to extend my sincere appreciation to the modern Masters of Edge Weapons for their immense pool of knowledge from which this body of information was derived for self-defense application.

*Grandmaster
Leovigildo M. Giron*

Guro Dan Inosanto

Guru Besar Herman Suwanda

Punong Guro Edgar G. Sulite and author.

Guro Dexter Labanog, Grandmaster Giron, Master Tony Somera

Steve Tarani is a full-time professional law enforcement trainer and is additionally available for private and group instruction for civilians. He can be reached at CONTACT DEFENSE AND CONTROL in California 949-515-0905 or click on www.contactdefense.com for additional information.

Author Steve Tarani instructing at Gunsite Academy.

About the Author

Steve Tarani lecturing on Contact Weapons at US Justice Training Center in Quantico, Virginia.

Steve Tarani, the nation's number one Contact Weapons Defensive Tactics Instructor, is a full-time professional law enforcement trainer, current Director and Primary Instructor for Contact Defense and Control (CA), on staff at the U.S. D.O.E. Nonproliferation and National Security Institute (Central Training Academy) Security Force Training Dept. at Kirtland Air Force Base (NM) and also on staff at the prestigious Gunsite Academy (AZ).

Steve Tarani began his training in edged weapons in 1979. Training extensively throughout the 1980's with the likes of Guro Ted Lucaylucay, and Grandmaster Leo M. Giron, Steve achieved his Graduate/Instructor ranking directly under Grandmaster Giron in Stockton, California, in1989. He is a long-term student of Guro Dan Inosanto and received instructorship directly under Guro Dan Inosanto in Los Angeles, California, in 1996. As a long-term private student of Punong Guro Edgar G. Sulite, Steve was also granted his instructorship in Palmdale, California, in 1997.

Subsequently, he is the only American to hold three simultaneous instructorships in the Filipino weapons arts respectively under Grandmaster Giron, Punong Guro Sulite and Guro Dan Inosanto.

Traveling to the source of "blade cultures" such as the Philippines, Japan and Indonesia, Steve took his intense training to the next level. After many years of research and investigation into the classical Chinese, Japanese, Filipino, Malaysian and Indonesian weapons systems, and extracting the essential and practical elements of application in modern urban defense against edged/ impact weapon attacks, Steve Tarani is unparalleled in his professionalism, teaching no-nonsense techniques that really work.

Steve is also a writer for various firearms training, law enforcement and martial arts magazines, has produced several videos and books, is a member of the American Press Association (APA), Inosanto Academy of Martial Arts Instructor's Association, Bakbakan International, LAMECO Eskrima International, Bahala Na Eskrima International and is a sworn deputy reserve for the state of Nevada.

Steve Tarani is currently available for seminars and can be reached for scheduling at (949) 515-0905 or via www.contactdefense.com or directly by e-mail at stevetarani@earthlink.net for more information.